SPAIN

By Nikos Kazantzakis

Translated by Amy Mims

CREATIVE ARTS BOOK COMPANY
BERKELEY / 1983

ISBN 0-916870-54-5

Library of Congress Card No. 63 15059

Manufactured in the United States of America.

CREATIVE ARTS BOOKS
ARE PUBLISHED BY
DONALD S. ELLIS

For more information contact:
Creative Arts Book Company
833 Bancroft Way
Berkeley, California 94710

■ CONTENTS

PUBLISHER'S NOTE

■ *The publishers and the translator of* Spain *are particularly grateful to Mr. Kimon Friar for his translation of Kazantzakis'* Don Quixote, *which appears between Parts I and II, and to Mr. Willis Barnstone of Indiana University for his translations of Spanish poetry.*

With the exception of the poems that have been translated from the Spanish, the text follows the Greek edition of Spain, *published by* ΔΙΦΡΟΣ, *Athens,* 1957.

PROLOGUE

■ PROLOGUE

■ TRAVELING AND CONFESSION (creation being the highest, most exact form of confession) have been my two greatest joys in life.

To wander over the earth; to see and never have my fill of seeing—new land and seas and men and ideas; to see it all as though for the first and the last time, with a long lingering gaze; and then to close my eyelids and feel the riches crystallizing inside me, calmly or tempestuously as they will, until Time has distilled them through its fine sieve into the quintessence of all my joys and all my griefs. This alchemy of the heart is, I believe, a great delight, worthy of Man.

For in this way, we not only come to know ourselves. Far, far more important, we are able to transcend our own insanely proud egos; plunging them and tempering them in the tormented itinerant army of Man.

I made several journeys, pirate voyages of my soul; outbursts of my aching heart; craving of my eyes that yearned and rushed to see as much water, as much earth as possible before their light would go out. I shall struggle to remember, by crushing the dry crust of logic enveloping my soul.

Every journey of mine, whether the cause or the result, marked some internal crisis in myself, where I felt stifled and could find no way out, except to die like a hero at the siege of Missolonghi. I believe that if I can capture all this in words, I shall be able to help shorten the agony of other kindred spirits who have set out along the same path.

I wish this confession to serve as a good deed. It wants no more than that. For I am not making Art. I am only letting my own heart cry out.

N.K.

pART i:
spAiN

◼ ON ENTERING SPAIN

◼ SPAIN HAS two faces. Its one profile, the elongated fiery visage of the Knight of the Woeful Countenance; and its other, the practical, square head of Sancho.

The whole brilliant vision of Spain wells up in my mind: the high plateaus of Castile and Estremadura, empty of water, empty of trees, rocks everywhere. The laughing hot valleys of Andalusia and Valencia, full of orange trees, lemon trees, bananas. The men dry and strong. The women with the tall towering combs in their perfumed hair and their black mantillas floating over them. Noise from the harbors and the bullfights and all the gaudy festivals. Arabic music droning with passion and death, floating up from the shady inner courtyards and the thick lattice windows of Cordova and Seville. Scents of jasmine, dung, rotting fruits. Mosques, cool churches, Moslem palaces. Crucified Christs along the riotous, colorful streets. Black-eyed little tramps of Murillo; dwarfs, bitter and proud, like those of Velázquez; Goyaesque beggars and gypsies; slender, reed-straight bodies of El Greco that flame like torches.

All Spain flooded with light, stirring inside my mind like a male peacock, its wings widespread, slowly strutting between two seas.

I closed my eyes so as to remember better. It had been raining gently, pleasantly. The Pyrenees were hidden in mist. A gay rainbow was suspended in the air, one tip touching the wild rocks of Spain, the other lost in the mist in the distance toward France.

Someone's back: straight, bony, proud. A bunch of onions hanging from the back and a guitar. Another back. . . . And another. . . . And another. Workmen's shirts, worn out, reeking of sweat, wine, garlic: human smells.

All of us: men, women, monks, crowded together at the border. The rain began to come down violently. A nun sitting next to me, silent and terribly pale, bit her lips. The starched white wings on her head were soaking wet now. They flopped down over her shoulders like doves that have just been killed. A plump peasant, wearing a thick red belt and a broad-brimmed hat, spat and cursed God for the rain.

A child near me started fussing and crying. His mother took a cabbage leaf out of a red sack and gave it to him. The boy calmed down and chewed away on the cabbage, blissfully, like a rabbit. A short workman with fiery eyes laughed and stretched out his hand. His wife handed him a big cabbage leaf too, then tied the sack tightly.

We all laughed, and I started up a conversation.

"Where're you coming from?"

"From France. We've been picking grapes in the French vineyards. Workmen. And you?"

"I'm a workman, too. In a different sort of vineyard."

He gave me a piece of cabbage. I too started chewing away. I became one with them. I felt at ease. The isolation that so annoys me when I am with literary people, the painful and at the same time arrogant joy I feel when I see the gulf separating man from man, here disappeared gently, effortlessly. A laugh; an insignificant conversation; a humble piece of cabbage; and the gulf was bridged.

Workmen, peasants, women wearing brightly colored shawls, monks, nuns. The rain was getting stronger, enveloping us all. A short, dark-haired Capuchin monk snarled:

"The Earth's going to wash away and punish us for our sins!"

A woman turned around, stared at him and laughed. She made some retort or other, but I couldn't hear it. Through the rain I could only see the glint of her teeth.

The light grew stronger. Our faces were bathed in light. Everyone's hats and hair and noses and umbrellas were dripping gently, like falling tears. But we felt a great joy at having arrived; at having set foot on Spanish soil; at having escaped the ironic, cutting eyes of the French.

There was a tired mother. She sat down on the bench at the station, opened her breasts and nursed her son. She opened her basket, brought out some bread, a bit of cheese, a large slice of melon, and ate them ravenously. She was refilling her veins, replenishing her empty breasts, silently, quickly transforming the bread, cheese, melon into milk.

The rain had stopped now. We could hear the waters running down from the surrounding mountains, full of stones. A yellow, muddy day: the mountaintops smiling, the birds shaking out their feathers; and we human beings, down below in the mud, happy because the clouds had scattered and we could see Spain before us, fragrant, freshly bathed, her harsh mountainsides sparkling in the sun.

Ah, the delight in seeing a village, a mountain, a rock, for the first time! The excitement of discovering all over the face of the earth the stubborn, indomitable effort of man to cultivate a tree, to build a hut, to take a wife and fill that hut with children!

I am struggling to spread out clearly in my own mind the whole, taut, bullskin shape of Spain on the world map. In my mind, I am carving her mountain ranges, her rivers and high plateaus and valleys. I am concentrating time: all the races that over the centuries passed over these plots of land and mixed their blood pass again in front of me—as though the mind were capable of holding the wheel of time and giving it a sudden impetus: Iberians, Celts, Phoenicians, Greeks, Carcadonians, Romans, Vandals, Visigoths, Arabs, Hebrews. Races mixed their blood and cast their flowers: warriors, wise men, poets, kings. Then at last the mystic fulfillment came, the profound synthesis, the hero of this whole land who fused all these ill-matched, ephemeral faces into one eternal face, so as to represent Spain at the great councils of time and space: the holy martyr Don Quixote. . . . And by his side, his mystic wife, Saint Teresa. The sacred couple of Spain.

Spain is the Don Quixote of nations. She rises up to save the earth, scorning security and well-being, forever hunting some exotic chimaera; never able to attain it. She exhausts herself in this quixotic, hyperrational campaign. Her cities are emptied. Her fields are left untilled. Her canals, built by the Arabs, are blocked and her gardens wither. She is creating her legend. What has she to do with happiness and comfort, with moderation and tranquillity? For many centuries the voice of Spain has been that of the fiery monk of Seville at the debate on what kind of temple to build: a large one or a small one. . . .

> *Let us build such a temple that*
> *they will take us for madmen!*

This has always been the resounding cry of life. Thus plants rose out of the mud, defying the laws of logic and gravity. Thus out of the grass sprang exotic beasts and flying creatures. Thus man too emerged from the beasts, walking upright on his hind legs, with a fiery spark inside his muddy skull. And so this Don Quixote cry against reason (which is, in actuality, the most profound longing for reason) reverberated among reasonable, practical human beings.

Happily absorbed in these reflections, I was watching Spain pass by outside my train compartment; to my right and left, the stones and fields and poor villages wedged in among the rocks. From time to time, a bell tower rising straight, watching over the houses. From time to time, a shepherd, consumed by the suns and rains, unmoving, his chin resting on his tall shepherd's staff and his infinite, eternal eye watching his skinny goats search vainly among the thistle-covered gray rocks.

Opposite me a young Spanish boy with small sparkling eyes was also gazing at Spain through the window of our train compartment. Our eyes met over the same stones and the same autumn-wounded vineyards. In a short time we were friends. Don Manuel was a modern-day Spaniard, an addict of the machine cult. His Mecca was New York City. Skyscrapers, airplanes, cinemas, jazz, sports, sex, a violent fast rhythm, a disdain for daydreams and art.

I feel happy when I see the younger generation scorning our old values and discovering new ones. I am happy, because thus I sense tangibly the enormous stride forward life has taken from my own youth to this other youth, the modern one. And I like this fast rhythm. I cannot bear secure, imperceptible motion. Before I die, I would like to see life move ahead as far as possible. So, what a joy it is to talk with a person younger than oneself; to see him laughing and jeering at the things people used to love in one's own youth! What a joy I feel that life is eager to leave me behind; no longer cares for me; is leaping toward other, young people; is attracted by other, dark heads! But I am not defeated or left behind, because I am not angry. Nor do I weep when I hear

the young men. Instead I laugh and jeer in company with
them.

I wanted to tease my young friend, to make him talk. The
Spaniard, like all children of the desert, is silent. To start
talking he must be excited, and then it is hard to stop him.
So I had to excite Don Manuel:

"Are we going to see Carmen?"

"Which Carmen?" he retorted nervously. "The one who
danced in a bolero and short dress, with castanets and a
blood-red rose in her hair? The one who drove the shameless
tourists mad? That's all done with! Now Carmen's a school-
teacher. She works as a factory employee and clamors for the
suffrage."

"And Don Quixote?"

"He's an engineer."

"But isn't he eternal?"

"He is. But he changes. In those days, he used to be a
knight. He read old folios and took a rusty sword. He wore
a barber's basin for a helmet and rode off on an ancient
horse to go out and save the world. Nowadays, he's an engineer. He's studied at the Technological Institute. He has
a diploma and practices his profession. He sees windmills and
knocks them down—with dynamite. He builds steam mills,
constructs roads, bridges, railway stations, airports. He's modern. He rides steam engines, automobiles, airplanes. Acham-
nontos is dead now and in the rubbish bin of Paradise!"

"So Don Quixote knows better now! Well, what good is
he then?"

"Of course, he's not spectacular any more. And the tourists who come to see him are just wasting their money. But
Spain is not a theatrical production. Nor are we extras dressed
up in medieval costumes. We are alive and modern. And so
our spirit, Don Quixote, is modern too. Who was Don Quixote

anyway? A hero who set out to save the world, armed with archaic weapons—shields and helmets. It was the time when the first guns and cannon had already been invented; the time when ideals and imagination had gone bankrupt; when personal gain, plunder, greed were rampant. But now Don Quixote knows better. He has turned practical. He wears heavy American glasses, wide comfortable shoes, a soft collar. He believes in machinery, in substantial matter, in happiness and swift pleasures. He gets mixed up in politics, proclaims freedom for the people. He's hard-working, a pacifist, slightly socialistic. He sacrifices everything for his ideals—everything except his own interest. Very rightly, too. Otherwise he would just end up again like the ancient roving troublemaker, who couldn't fit in any place!"

"And Dulcinea?"

"She's changed, too. She's come down out of the clouds of the imagination. She's come up from her humble village, and now she's living in Madrid. She's married to the modern Don Quixote and has become a housewife. She cooks, washes, quarrels, has children. She's changed her name too."

"What's her name now?"

"Democracia."

I was looking at the trees and earth. Little stations; sudden voices; women wearing all sorts of shawls; old women who looked as though they were hewn out of the knobby wood of olive trees. Life here is very harsh. All this earth is kneaded with sweat and tears. I turned to my friend:

"Well, long live Don Sancho!"

"That's the great mistake all foreigners make. Quixote and Sancho are one. Both of them together form the single unified spirit of Spain. Cervantes divided our spirit into two parts, so that we could see it better. The Spanish spirit is a rich unity, for inside our dry, hard shell, two antithetical forces embrace each other like twin almonds. The Spaniard knows that Dulcinea exists only inside himself. He knows that justice, freedom, the ideal also exist only inside himself. But he reflects: 'Perhaps what exists inside ourselves is the only truth? The only reality? Perhaps everything the practical man sees and touches is deception and a dream?'

" 'Only the desire inside ourselves is real and alive!' proclaims the one peak of the Spanish spirit.

" 'Only what we see and touch is real and alive!' proclaims the other peak of the Spanish spirit—Sancho. 'What you're saying, master, is just *palabras*—just words!'

"This is the genuine, deep-rooted struggle of Don Quixote —and so of Spain. The Spanish spirit is quixotic-sanchoesque or sancho-quixotic, according to the season. Sometimes the one age-old element is dominant, sometimes the other. But always they are struggling and suffering together. Don't be surprised by the skyscrapers you'll see in Madrid, or by our economic and political concerns. Behind this modern-day, coarse, sanchoesque façade emerges—you have only to know how to look for it—the saintlike, grief-worn face, luminous and ecstatic, of the great patron of Spain—Don Quixote. You see, even I—the prosaic man, the mechanical modern man . . . You scratched Sancho a bit and out of me leaped Don Quixote."

I didn't say anything. I was remembering the wise Moslem mathematician and poet, Abu-Ali, who was continually in love. All women pleased him equally and he couldn't decide which one to choose. "All women," he writes in one of his songs, "form a circle around me. My heart is the center, and thence the rays of my love shoot forth like arrows that are always equal."

The heart of the free thinker is like this too. All the aspects of his thinking are equally well loved by him, the sad or happy masks of the same desire.

■ MIRANDA

■ PEACEFUL AND MUDDY, the Ebro River winds her way through the lonely, unsmiling plain. Gray clods of soil; trees that have lost their leaves; no bird or gay color. A severe, forbidding landscape. The one aspect of Spain, the unsmiling one. Further down on the sun-washed shores of the Mediterranean, or in the Oriental gardens of Andalusia, we take delight in the other face of Spain, the laughing face.

On the banks of the Ebro, the poor huts of Miranda stand crowded together. Narrow dirty streets; primitive carts carrying dung; men with harsh features; dried-up women. I moved through the narrow lanes, gazing slowly and lingeringly, greeting and bidding farewell to the miserable low huts and dry trees and dusty windows. Suddenly a tiny church to Saint Nicholas made my heart beat faster. Once upon a time it had been an Arab mosque. Surely, here in front, there must have been a courtyard and a little fountain and green trees. There might also have been a jasmine plant and two or three pairs of doves. But the monk had come and chased them away. The cupola, that graceful curve rising from the ground and falling back to the ground, had turned into an ascetic Gothic arch with stone trees, stone flowers and stone doves. The arrow had left the earth, rushed into the sky and no longer wanted to return.

I wandered around the little church, content that my heart was not able to choose. This desperate quixotic assault on

23

Heaven, even if it is empty, is good. But it is also good to wage an everlasting campaign on the green earth. I could see carvings eaten away by time on the walls. An elegant, strong Gothic arch formed the doorway. The windows were divided in the middle by tiny columns, the top of each tiny column being a saint's head. One of these heads had an amazingly expressive forcefulness: heavy cheekbones, forehead, cheeks, chin, cut in broad planes; thick, lowered eyelids; lips full of passion and bitterness.

My heart beat violently. I stopped short. This was our ancient grandam, Africa; the hot dark land of our ancestors, full of rubbery-leaved trees and starving wild beasts. How was it that this savage thick-lipped African mask was suddenly confronting me in this old Spanish town so far to the north? Some Negro renegade must have carved it. His mind had set out to hew a Christian ascetic, but the ancestors inside him had resisted and guided his hand.

And so in the inner recesses of this dry and virtuous church, we find this lascivious Negro mask stuck in, breathing desires and lust for the flesh. For a moment the church trembled, dissolved, and its light went out in the pale autumn sun. A forest lay there in front of me, full of beasts and brightly colored birds and hungry merciless gods who had climbed up to sit on the highest trees. They were laughing. All day long the men worked in the sun. As soon as the sun set, the earth echoed with drumbeats and wild dances and the shrill screams of hunted women. People spoke with the gods and the beasts, with the water and the snakes. The whole world was a rich, colorful, teeming vision. Divine intoxication made their temples throb. And heroic song soared upward, free of useless frills, harsh and laconic.

The human soul is like that small devilish dancer in an African song, "Bana Bayinda" . . .

A woman gave birth in the desert, underneath a tree. It was a female child. It was raining, raining on the mother and the child. The mother died. It went on raining, raining on the child all night long till daybreak. The child lay beneath the tree. Three years the child lay beneath the tree. Then, suddenly, she shook herself and rose and began to sing:

"I am a woman whom everyone loves. I am a woman the devil loves too. I am a woman whom God loves. I am a woman the people love. My name is Bana Bayinda."

The girl started on her way. She reached a city and began to sing. All the people cried: "Such a song as this we've never heard!" Three times again Bana Bayinda danced that night. Suddenly she screamed loud and fell on the bullskin, dead.

For centuries now, this lustful bitter mask in the church has been watching Bana Bayinda dance. It has stared down on what my own small heart also yearns day and night, insatiably, to watch: this dancer who lived so little time; life; bitterness; joy; incurable vanity.

Sadly I tore myself away from this mask. I would never see it again. But I felt happy that I had seen it suddenly in this way, in a lonely plain of Castile, and had left on its thick lips an invisible drop of blood.

I moved back and forth among the narrow little streets. An old peasant was unloading his wagon full of hay. The old woman in the doorway opened both panels of the door for him. It was a heavy load and the old man stumbled. I ran to help him and we picked up a conversation.

"How're you getting along with the Democracy now, old man?"

The old man shrugged his bony shoulders. "Same as always. We're poor . . ."

"Hungry?"

"Eh, of course. Can't you see us? Skin and bones! Just look at my old woman here. A scarecrow. She's a broomstick."

The old woman laughed.

"It's better that way, childie. 'Course it is. What's the good of fattening up my flesh for the worms to get at? All the flesh they find is theirs, but my bones are my own. They can't eat them off me. And I can last a thousand years!"

The old man shoved his old wife.

"Come on now, Teresina—stop your chatter and come help me!"

The old woman took the bundle of hay in her arms with the same strength with which she must have once embraced her husband. She took two steps toward the courtyard, then turned around laughing:

"Where are you from, *caballero?*"

"From very far away."

"And why did you come here?"

"To look!"

"What's there to look at, you poor boy! Why didn't you stay in your own place? Everywhere's the same. What's the good of it? It's not worth anything. Everything belongs to Death."

Everything belongs to Death! *Nada, nada.* Nothing, nothing! The most profound, most characteristic outcry of the Spanish spirit: their awareness of the Nothing—that life is a dream. From the humblest peasant up through Calderón and Cervantes resounds this profound and tragic conviction that life is a dream: *Let us dream, O my soul, let us dream.*

The Spaniard, except for his moments of sudden, demonic energy, looks with an Oriental eye upon the spectacle of the world. The peasant says goodbye to his own people, boards the train, off to sail perhaps for America. Out of the train window, he looks at his relatives and shakes his head, murmuring: "How far away they are already! How far!" His parents, children, friends, the village where he was born, already seem to him lost in the foggy mist of recollection. Reality becomes rarefied and refined inside his mind—undulating, colorful, far off, mysterious like a dream.

Many virtues of the Spaniard spring from this passive conception of reality. Above all, his profound, intense humanitarianism. The more visionary the Spaniard is, the more he lives the destiny of all humanity as his own personal destiny. The world's adventure becomes his own individual adventure. In this the Spaniard's soul is very like the Russian's: he has the same ability to feel sympathy, to become one with other people. "Yes, yes, I dream," Calderón proclaims in his play, *Life Is a Dream*. "I dream and I want to do good. For any action that is good cannot be lost, even in the dream."

And there is another virtue of the Spaniard—his stoicism—rooted in his divination that all reality, warp and woof, is but a dream. The spectacle of the vanity of life, the suspicion that everything's a dream, give him heroic powers of resistance, a calm smile, a proud, mute patience. The Spaniard is not melodramatic. He does not lament. He does not shout. He does not lower himself by giving way to useless complaining. Just as when we have a bad dream, and in our sleep we are aware that it is a dream and so take courage and are not upset by it, so the Spaniard, even while he is alive, seems to be aware of what life is: a dream that will fade away. And so he takes courage in the midst of disaster and does not collapse.

The Spaniard's way of thinking is in harmony with his spirit. The Spaniard reflects on his life, both external and internal, waiting for the Idea to emerge of itself. He has an extraordinarily acute power of perception, but no critical ability. He is able to make a synthesis, and he does so with great joy, as though it alone is worthy of him. But any critical analysis he undertakes with difficulty and distaste. In temperament and spirit the Spaniard is fantastically well qualified. But he lacks method, technique, the patience for meticulous revision. "The Spaniard," says a Castilian proverb, "either gallops like a horse or, like a mule, stands still." He finds it very disagreeable, contrary to his nature, to move ahead at a calm regular pace.

Noontime. I moved out of the little city into the fields. Mud; desolation as far as the eye could reach; no smoke or house or passer-by. I like Spain, because her warm feminine gardens are flanked by these inhuman wastelands. Boundless plains and high plateaus whence the waters have vanished, rivers that have changed their course, leaving only sand and granite in their wake. Naked, stripped of flesh and clothes and ornaments, the skeleton of the earth . . .

A splendid smithy for the souls of heroes. Here of necessity, the spirit is forged as in the vast wastelands of broiling heat or icy cold. Solitude, no help anywhere, and bad luck to any man who breaks. In the desert one learns to be self-sufficient; to expect help from no one—neither God nor man nor beast nor tree nor water. On the one side there is oneself, and on the other, all the dark cannibalistic forces of earth and heaven. A moment's weakness and one is lost. There are no neighbors here, no relatives, no police force. One is alone. Except that a step in back of one, dogging one's heels, Death is following, day and night. One has no other companion.

So the spirit grows brave, learns willy-nilly, that fear is a mortal weakness and that from only one person can salvation be expected: oneself. Only this remains faithful. Life is tragic. It is not pleasure or a game or a point of departure for philosophers' and aesthetes' theories. It is a struggle. Eat or be eaten. Life is a tigress that has tasted human flesh, found it utterly delicious and now hungers for it insatiably. She enters villages and cities and, wherever she finds a human being, snatches him. There is no flesh more delicious.

This is how spirits are fashioned in the boundless waste-lands: in Spain, in Africa, at the Poles. I remember racing over a terrifying snowy desert in a Laplander's sleigh. The reindeer pulling it gleamed like crystal. We climbed a hill, and from its crest, far off in all directions, I was face to face with unending snow, inimical, empty of human or animal breath. It was evening. My heart contracted and I turned to my apathetic silent guide:

"Aren't you afraid?" I asked him in Russian.

"No."

"Why? You have your hopes in God?"

The Laplander shook his head slowly. "God is very high up. He can't see or hear."

"Then why aren't you afraid?"

"If I'm afraid, I'm lost!"

"If I'm afraid, I'm lost!" How many centuries were needed till the desert could communicate to people this practical and heroic formula for success! No refuge in gods, demons, abstract conceptions. No appeal to the nobility and pride of man. In danger, the most advantageous policy is not to fear. Only thus is it possible to preserve one's powers intact, to struggle and have the best possible chance of not being de-stroyed. No other method is profitable.

This sublime lesson in courage is well known to the Span-iard. His own wastelands have taught it to him. The genuine

Spaniard, the man who created the Spanish epic, is a child of the desert. An individualist, proud, courageous, and at the same time possessing all the weaknesses of this great virtue; he is incapable of working with others, of following a common program, of undertaking in a disciplined way any work that requires much time and labor. He is One. Captain Sole! When his passion fuses him momentarily with others, he accomplishes incredible exploits. But quickly his passion sputters out and the Spaniard withdraws into his tower—into his own soul. Alone, Captain Sole, a bit of mosaic that refuses to, or, rather, that cannot combine with other bits of mosaic, subjected to the scheme of a single grand mosaic larger than the individual: "Yo! Yo! I! I!" Here is the hoarse persistent cry, torn out of the vitals of Spain. "I! I!" cries her most perfect representative nowadays: Don Miguel Unamuno. "I, no one else! And not only in this life: in the other one as well. I do not want the abstract-characterless, beyond-character immortality of the Europeans. I want the genuine, the only immortality worthy of my Spanish soul. I must survive, I, myself, Unamuno, Don Miguel Unamuno, with this flesh of mine, these twenty nails of mine, and my own pointed quivering goatee!"

■ BURGOS

■ CASTILE: "THE FORTRESS." This whole illustrious region, entered on crossing the Ebro, has indeed been the fortress—the stone heart—of Spain. And Burgos, this austere military city, was Castile's head. From this eagle's nest the counts and kings of León and Castile set forth to chase the Arabs from Spanish soil. Here was born the Spaniards' Digenes Akritas,* Ruy Díaz de Bivar, the Cid. And here took place his famous wedding to Ximena.

Ruins of aristocratic houses; uphill and downhill lanes; the Arlanzón River flowing through the heart of the city. Public gardens have been planted along its banks and in the evening the good citizens, the wrathless descendants, take their peaceful strolls there and discuss politics. The rhythm of life has calmed down. The heroic Burgos has survived like a magnificent sheath, full of carvings and dates, but empty of a sword.

Like the fox investigating the lion's den, I wandered around, but did not enter the huge Gothic cathedral.

A military fortress: dark, with turrets and loopholes and scalding pots, from which they used to pour the boiling water and oil to burn the besiegers. The "sweet" Christ has reverted to His harsh, irreconcilable form as Jehovah. He has donned His panoply again—all of stone here—and taken His stand at the borders to fight the Infidels.

---

* The medieval Greek champion of chivalry.

Recall the tears and supplications of Saint Francis of Assisi, the "little beggar," the "pauper of God," as he liked to be called. He was already an old man. His band had begun to flourish when his harsh pupil Elias took the reins out of the kind, trembling hands of the master and began to build the magnificent, three-story monastery of Saint Francis in Assisi. He filled it with precious wall paintings, gilded Bibles, many-colored stained-glass windows. "This is not the stable of our Christ!" Francis protested unhappily. "This is a palace, a fortress! I do not want it! I do not want it!" And the coarse Elias winked at the brothers, pointed toward the saint in whose honor the temple had been built and muttered: "He's in his dotage!"

God, born among slaves, burrowed and hid Himself like a mole in the catacombs. After a while, the slaves grew strong, freed themselves, rose up from the underground passages, occupied the palaces. And God grew strong with them, was freed, rose up from the dark dungeons, and made His throne in palaces and fortresses. These enormous churches are a testimony not to the power of God, but to the power and faith and pride of man. Such is the Cathedral of Burgos. A military impregnable fortress, a lion's cave, the lair of some pre-cataclysm monster.

I crossed the threshold with a shudder, groping forward slowly in the half-light. Once again I felt that turmoil and ecstasy which Gothic churches arouse in me. The high up-right arches, the stone tresses, the pointed domes, the blue, dense darkness hovering in the corners, the magic sparkle cast by the cool colors of the stained-glass windows—all ruby, topaz, emerald.

The Spirit had blown and the rocks had been raised and all these stone marvels rose and remained floating in the air. The grand periods of creation are an insoluble mystery. In the midst of the harshest medieval wars, deprived of comfort and security and amid daily dangers, the creators painted and sang and wrote and built churches and wrought stone or iron. Apparently the forces of the Spirit, good or bad, are all aroused and grow strong simultaneously. Whether for good or bad, out of imperceptible variations, it is possible to produce a wretched, cowardly soul. Everything is orgasm and power and desire and is capable of becoming Spirit. The only accursed barren existence is the miserly one—that which does not spend, does not pursue danger, does not desire, satisfied only with the base tranquillity of moderation and comfort.

To be sure, great works are also born in peacetime. But what kind of peace? The daughter of war. For the seed falls during the erotic moment of war, then later becomes visible and grows in the years of peacetime. The Crusaders went to the East to deliver the Holy Sepulchre, so they thought. But actually they went in order to deliver the forces they had inside themselves. Their eyes luxuriated in calm seas, sun, date trees, mosques, peacocks. Their fingers vibrated as they touched silk carpets, as they caressed dark-haired Eastern women. And when they returned to their own countries, their memory was flooded with good things and their sacks were full of gold and ivory, manuscripts with miniatures, silk embroideries, holy relics. They had acquired new senses. And now as they touched the stones, the stones came to life—became vines, animals, chimaeras. Windows opened in the dusky churches like roses in the northern mist.

I entered this fortress of God stealthily, like a spy creeping into an enemy camp to try and dislocate its secret fortification works. I stared at each decoration attentively, and when no one was watching, stretched my hand out to touch them. In the heart of the temple lay the tombstone of the travel-stained rapacious Akritas of Spain, and, by his side, his faithful, long-suffering wife. In a golden niche, lit with a row of torches and silver candles, stood a large life-size Christ, made of skin and real hair. Coming from the East, as tradition has it, it was the work of Nicodemus, who made it by copying the actual body of Christ. The Crusaders brought it here, dressed it in a white lace robe, fitted on it a wig made of human hair, left the chest bare and streaming with blood.

So in this Cathedral the two heroes met who perfectly embody the aspirations of the Spanish soul, the two opposite extremes: one, the Cid—hardiness, bravery, violence, the masculine expression of life—and by his side, Christ crucified —suffering, patience, sacrifice, femininity. The one a few steps from the other. As the Spaniard walks these few steps, his soul strides from its one pole to its other.

The Spaniard's religion is no abstract, fleshless dogma, no distant intellectual contact with an unapproachable God. It is a warm embrace, a hand and a wound, the hand of man plunged into the wound of God. And for the Spaniard, the Madonna is no inaccessible Virgin treading on white clouds. She's like one of the little peasant girls from Andalusia or Castile, sitting on her doorstep at eveningtime, spinning—or as the Andalusian folk song has it:

"The Madonna is down a-washing her little baby's linen, among the rosemary."

The Spaniards love Christ because He is crucified; because He is suffering; because they can see His blood flowing in five streams from His five wounds. That is why the Spaniards so love the deep-carved wooden statues with their flamboyant colors, their scarlet blood, their tears as thick as kidney beans, their deep gaping wounds. In Spain one rarely sees "Resurrections," happy saints, God in triumph. Such a God has no need of us. How could our prayer reach Him? But the crucified Christ is near us, is one of us. He lacks but a little to be human like us. Every woman becomes a *Pietà*, holding her unjustly murdered son in her arms.

In the shadowy light of the Cathedral, I contemplated the women kneeling and praying for hours on end, their wrists crossed, like crucified figures themselves. Other women came in from the market with their shopping in their hands: vegetables, a melon, a fishtail sticking out of their baskets. They held them tightly, like their own child, and stared at the Christ on bended knees, overcome by feeling. Surely in a moment all women are transformed to mothers mourning their child. This is their oldest, deepest aspect, most truly their own. But here in Spain the expression on their faces is more primitive, more bitter. The face of the Spanish woman seems to have recaptured its genuine hypersensual essence: suffering and death. How God becomes man inside the womb of woman, this simplest of mysteries, one sees here in Spain with a shudder of awe.

A smooth-cheeked candlelighter beckoned to me in the dark. He was a crafty old man, dressed in a violet smock like a cardinal. His hands shook hastily, nervously, bright yellow:

"Come 'ere! Come 'ere!"

"What do you want?"

"Come 'ere!"

He dragged me over to a big wooden door to show me the carved birds and animals and flowers. The wood was deep black, hard and fine like iron. Joy in life; delight in detail; an ebullient passion; a bird stretching its neck upward, singing near the doorlock as though longing to open it with his song. I looked at the candlelighter. Short and cunning, with a wiry cold voice like a eunuch's. His ancestors had carved this wood. Their spirit had blown on this door, was still alive, was still blowing and rumpling my hair. The man stretched his withered yellow hand out to me now and begged me for a penny.

The Spirit had passed here once upon a time, creating heroic acts, great works of art, momentous thoughts. The Spirit had whipped the lazy, cowardly human soul and forced it to leap. The Spirit had set fire to the straw which the mind, like an ant, had been gathering over the ages. The flame had leaped up and the whole of Spain had sparkled with its reflection. Then when it had done its duty of burning, the Spirit had fled, leaving in its wake the charred remains.

Well then, will the Spirit pass here again? Does the Spirit ever pass twice over the same race and the same place? "Debtor-races," as Spengler cruelly dubbed the nations that had created great civilizations but once: the Egyptians, Assyrians, Persians, Indians. At that moment, as I watched the Spanish candlelighter in the semidarkness, with his withered outstretched hand, I felt terrified. A few centuries earlier, in this same place, another hand—his ancestor's—full of fury and joy, all-powerful, was struggling with substance, forcing wood and stone to assume all the forms of the human soul —bird, tree, God.

How long had this breath of creation lasted? Apparently, opposed to the laws of the earth, it was swiftly quenched. The Spirit is unable to remain aloft for a long time and falls back on the ground, returning to its real base. I have often heard the conceited geese in our own country proclaiming and writing: "The climate, the sky, the light, the line of Greece . . . Where could the Spirit find better conditions for building its nest and entrusting its eggs?" But they forget that the climate and sky and light and line of Greece were the same for thousands of years, yet only for a moment —two or three centuries—did the Spirit build its nest there.

And then it flew elsewhere, where there was no such sun, no blue sky, to build its nest in the cold and mist.

"Debtor-races!" Sometimes a cruel thought sweeps through me tempestuously. Wherever the Spirit has passed once, it will never pass again. The carnivorous bird never returns to its old nest.

The candlelighter grabbed his penny and disappeared in the darkness. As soon as I was by myself, I caressed the carvings on the door to see them better. My hand stopped short at the singing bird: its hard neck, open beak, powerful, hooklike claws. . . . I seemed to be touching and caressing the spirit of the ancient carver, as though I had resurrected the great endeavor inside myself. Suddenly I felt tremendous joy in this carved bird. It seemed to me suddenly that national entities had been transcended and that all the changeable nests of the unstable birdlike spirit are really built in the human heart. And so the bloodstained endeavor of the Spirit, in whatsoever field of the earth, is a universal human endeavor that bursts out and goes on indestructibly inside every human being who continues the struggle.

It was evening by the time I escaped from the lion's den. I went back to the uphill streets and walked along the banks of the yellow-green river. For a moment the setting sun came into sight among the clouds. Sparkling light on the people's faces. The illustrious old coats-of-arms: lions, eagles, chimaeras, bathed in light over the lintels of the rickety villas. In the old days some seven centuries ago, during the frenzied orgasm of creation, this whole city—towers, workshops, market places, human souls—had worked with godlike unity. Together they had erected the watchtower of their God in the midst of their own homes: their cathedral. Nowadays towers, workshops, market places, human souls, have fallen in ruins, and only the vast stone lair of the serpent remains—empty.

A large square hummed with the noise of throngs of playing children. Round about, poor little shops selling fruits and coal; saddle shops; inns; horseshoeing shops; a keen smell of mules and people. And as backdrop to the square, the superb old palace where Queen Isabella received the grand martyr Columbus, after his triumphant return from discovering the New World.

There was a high door trimmed with a thick stone pattern, woven like the figurehead of a ship. It had lions as sentinels and turrets at the four corners. In the empty courtyard the flagstones were all uprooted and covered with grass. I restrained my imagination from flooding with easy illusions: how Columbus had entered through this door and filled the courtyard with all his colorful motley cortege. Columbus, "Don Quixote of the sea . . ." All this courtyard, so overgrown with grass now, once must have teemed with rainbow-colored birds and exotic beasts, with unknown plants, mysterious fruits, thick lumps of gold. Like a carnival of History, but now a desert. Two sparrows were chasing each other around the columns. An old fleabitten dog lifted its head, looked at me, but was too weak to bark. I moved back and forth in the ruined courtyard, like its landlord. "The transparent chronicles of the air," as the great Góngora phrased it, have now faded away. Only the fires made by living children and the thuds of the horseshoe maker and the smell of horse manure remain.

At daybreak the next morning, I left hurriedly to catch the train. The Cathedral rose angry and threatening beneath the great stars of dawn.

■ VALLADOLID

■ THE ALTITUDE was rising as we advanced along the high ascetic plateau of Castile. Now and then a hungry crow passed by. Now and then a village perched up on the shoulders of the mountain, hardly visible, like a heap of stones set among the other stones of the Sierra de Guadarrama. A tiny church floating on a peak, the two edges of its roof slanting sharply upward, like a Moslem tomb or a sacrificial horn from Knossos. A slender goat, also gray, stepped out from behind a cleft rock, then stopped still. An old peasant clambered up the dry river bed. He was squarely built, rough-hewn, eaten by the rains and the sun. He had a thin shaved mustache and a huge jawbone. I had never been so deeply aware of how much everything—mountains, trees, animals, human beings, ideas—in each given place, is made of the surrounding material.

I stared at the stones, breathed in the Castilian air, longing to see far off in the distance some ruined windmill. I sensed that we had arrived in the mad, ruined duchy of the great prince, Don Quixote. Here in this prophetic steppe he was the grand feudal lord. Here the Knight of the Ideal (the wilderness) set forth to free slaves, give justice to those who were unjustly treated, protect orphans and widows, pay the debts and fight the base passions of the world—jealousy, injustice, fear, dishonesty, laziness, arrogance.

The daydreamer, unwilling to be delivered from his dream,

set forth among these wild uninhabitable mountains in search of the chimaera. Among such rocks as these, in summertime when the winds whistle over the stones, the boundaries of the dream and the truth vacillate and are lost. The brain seethes and feels confused and thinks all things easy for an energetic willing spirit. Our hearts stop. We see him coming out the back door of the proud beggar's tower and we want to shout to him: "Where are you going, beloved one, with that old moribund horse of yours, and your rusty spear, your lost youth, your money belt empty of gold ducats and not a drop of common sense in you? Come back!" But the fearless simple lover of the Idea and of the heartless Dulcinea was already down in the plain, had already raised his spear. He was all love and wrath. The world had emerged from God's hands, rife with injustice and shortcomings. And he, the Knight of the Ideal, was duty-bound to set it right. For Don Quixote's work begins where God's leaves off.

The whole terrible endeavor begins, amid laughter and tears, the windmills, sheep, serpents and dragons, thrashings, hunger, and finally the humiliating unbearable return. Our laughter is more bitter than our tears, for at the very moment we are laughing at the great Spirit in his agony, we are deeply aware of how abominable this life is, which rewards only mediocre calculating schemes and scorns generous noble enterprises.

Imagine how the Spaniards, around 1600, must have reacted to this comic mask of their own tragic spirit. Behind this mask they could see Spain herself as clear as day. For like the frenzied hero of La Mancha, Spain too had launched out, impoverished and exhausted, but full of imagination, on behalf of a great idea: to save the world by spreading Christianity. Spain too was governed by the saintly madness of Don Quixote. She too could not distinguish the dream from the reality. And then one August evening in 1588 the awful news arrived: the invincible Armada had been demolished off the rocky coasts of England. All Spain fell, never to rise again; for with the Armada sank all her quixotic dreams. Don Quixote and Spain went back to their ruined old tower, humbled and ready to die.

Exactly at this period, one man was experiencing all this tragic adventure of his country within his own small frame: Cervantes.

He too had launched forth full of dreams. As a young man of twenty-four, he had fought heroically at Návpaktos. Then he'd fallen ill, and the commanders, when they saw him shaking with fever, refused to take him in the battle. Cervantes, already carried away by Don Quixotesque passion, shouted: "What does my fever matter? I'll still fight bravely! Better that I should die fighting for Christ and the king, than stretched out on my own mattress! Give me the most dangerous post, and I swear to stand by it and die fighting!" In the same way, with the same feverish excitement and faith, Don Quixote also spoke. And Spain also spoke! Well, they did take him and he fought bravely. He was wounded again, but rushed back into battle. When he returned to his own country, he expected the king to welcome him with open arms. He expected honors and titles. But not a soul turned to look at him. In despair, he plunged into writing. "I shall write great works!" he proclaimed. "I shall win glory and riches! With my pen I shall gain what I could not gain with my sword!" He threw himself onto paper, writing away furiously —theatrical works and narrations. But glory did not come. Nor was his heart fulfilled. He was passionately in love with a woman who discarded him because he was poor and insignificant. She married another man.

Cervantes was in despair. More than forty years old now, he abandoned his pen and plunged into practical life, as a merchant. He became a provisioner for the Armada, and traveled around Spain buying oil and wheat for the fleet. The Armada sank, and with it Cervantes went bankrupt. He tried to leave secretly for America, but they seized him and threw him into debtors' prison. In prison Cervantes sat contemplating his life. He had started out to become a hero by fighting the Infidels. He had not succeeded. Then he had set out to become a great poet and write immortal works. He had not succeeded. Then he had loved a woman, and she had betrayed him. Attracted by trade, he'd been thrown into debtors' prison. What had he gained? For what purpose was all this bloodstained adventure of his life? How had he started, with what dreams, and now where had he ended up! An old man, without any money, without friends, without glory, a comic wreck of a ship that had sallied out to conquer the world. Was this not just what his own great country had also suffered? By around 1600, they both had cast anchor, shipwrecked in the landlocked still waters of moderation.

And then at the brink of despair, there in prison, inside Cervantes' bitter heart, Don Quixote was born. He put the dreams of his own youth and the dreams of Spain's youth into the old knight's wind-blown brain, and sent him out to battle with terrifying merciless reality. He laughed and wept with Don Quixote's sufferings, for they were his own sufferings. And with him, all Spain laughed and wept too, for it was she herself who had set out with just such a paper panoply, just such a great idea, only to return wounded in a hundred places.

The Spaniards, exhausted and no longer able to launch grand campaigns that defied logic and prudence, were delighted to read this tale, for it expressed for them the fu-

tility and absurdity of every movement. Spain loved Don
Quixote because she no longer had any belief. With joy she
saw that perhaps the absence of an ideal was the best way of
bringing her people safely to reality, without any dangerous
quirks. Don Quixote consoled the great Castilian spirit in its
downfall. Art could not have given a more precious gift to
Spain at this critical moment of her unbearable sadness.

Here, on these mountains I was traveling through today,
the eternally roving Knight of the Ideal suffered and fought.
In company with Ulysses and Hamlet and Faust, he is
rooted in the souls of men. These are the four ruling princes
of human souls. In the others' legions may be found the
keenest, cleverest of men, or the most fastidious and delicate,
or the greatest conquerors. But closest to Don Quixote's
heart are the soldiers (young recruits and old veterans alike),
deeply, bitterly, eternally close to him. For perhaps of all the
princes, Don Quixote most faithfully mirrors the fate of
man.

So in the shadow of our great prince I entered Valladolid,
the heart of Castile. This ancient capital of Spain, with its
splendid churches and huge abandoned palaces, is like a
fallen princess whose lovers have all died, and so she has had
to take to industry and commerce in order to survive.

Great kings loved her. Cardinals remained true to her unto
death. But all this grandeur is spurned by any traveler capable of remembering and distinguishing the ephemeral from
the eternal, by anyone who can catch the essence of a place.
Only one thing remains from Valladolid, one memory: a
tiny, poor house, damp, overgrown with ivy, with dark windows and iron grillwork. This little house is the heart of Valladolid, all that is most precious in her, for inside it lived
and suffered a great creator: Cervantes. Thus the Spirit is
avenged on all the ephemeral grandeur that so plagued it

during its passage over the earth when it was pinioned to a human head.

I felt tremendously moved as my eyes encompassed this house. They were loath to tear themselves away. Here they encompassed the whole tempestuous life of a person who had been able to define clearly the spirit of his race and so save it from compromise and destruction. Magic the power of speech that is capable of creating the thing, or of enclosing the created thing within clearly defined limits, so that it cannot overflow or shrink and lose its original form. Perhaps Quevedo, Cervantes' contemporary, is a more powerful writer—richer, cleverer, more forceful, with his broad humor and pathos and his violent love of life. But in none of his works could he immortalize the twofold essence of the Spanish spirit. Not capable of saving, he was not saved. But Cervantes, with his Don Quixote and his Sancho, saved the spirit of his race from being destroyed by time, and he too was saved along with her. Dante, centuries after his death, effected the unification of Italy by having coerced her in his strict *terza rima* to be a united Italy. Just so, Cervantes expressed in speech the hidden or still unfathomed characteristics of his race. He made them crystal-clear and fixed, and the Spaniards, seeing this most perfect expression of themselves, were coerced into conforming to their own racial character. Such is the difficult, dangerous, utterly mysterious responsibility of the great creator.

Another creator of Valladolid and Spain is the wood carver Gregory Hernandez, who was all passion and power. Here in Valladolid he carved in wood the tragic funeral procession of the Crucifixion—the bandits and Roman soldiers; the Incense Bearers and the common people, jeering and ridiculing the naked Christ, who is pale and bathed in blood. Here are all the Sancho types: people of the flesh, heavy eaters and drinkers with thick sagging lips and mocking eyes, some innocent, some wily. And along with them, all the Don Quixote types: the slender, palpitating, terrified apostles; the heroic, powerless women; and at the high peak of reality and imagination, the Grand Martyr—the Don Quixote of heaven, with His crown of thorns.

The wood is brilliantly colored. The expression is so powerfully realistic and the mouths, eyes, lips, arms so alive that we are filled with awe. Time seems to have turned back, casting us down on the dusty, bloody uphill path in Jerusalem. The Divine Passion is brought back to life. The mob, as always, rushes forth to kill its Saviour. These colored wooden statues embody eternal ideas. The Spanish craftsman has instilled into them all the fire, movement, and oil paints necessary for making the Passion intelligible to Spanish spirits. Streams of blood gush from Christ's wounds. The Spaniard, who loves blood, feels exalted as he sees it, and his oldest, deepest virtue is aroused. He is ready to set forth, ignoring ridicule and death, to save the world. To the Spaniard, is Jesus Christ perhaps but another aspect, the most pathetic, the most hidden and sacred, of Don Quixote?

Today, as I touched these colored idols which head the Easter Week processions, I recalled, involuntarily, the other mystic rite that so profoundly stirs the Spaniards: bullfighting. These two rites became inseparably fused inside me. Perhaps the killing of the bull in the religion of Mithra had the same meaning as the sacrifice of Christ-Amnos in the Christian religion? Was it not perhaps the same primitive universal human instinct that drove the sacred bullfighter of Mithra to kill his god?

Valladolid has many old churches heavily laden with stone saints, Virgins, chimaeras, birds. Here the baroque style bursts out with all its unbearable lavishness and bombast. The classical column has reverted to its original undisciplined form, is once again an overbearing tree. All the seeds of this chaotic uncontrolled orgasm of the baroque hatched, ripened, and were disseminated without discipline or finesse. Bodies suffocated in clothes—clothes that are blown back and forth by a frantic wind—eyes, hands, feet, at their most violent paroxysm. There is no empty space in between these bodies, no relief. There is no silence. In spite of ourselves, we long for the calm and nobility and balance of the classical discipline. Here in Valladolid, I observed this unbridled spirit in the paintings and statues with silent antipathy. Surely the highest art is passion that is controlled; order in the midst of chaos; serenity both in joy and pain. To be master of ourselves; to be master of the material we are using in order to express ourselves; not to be seduced by extraneous beauties; not to be won over by the notion that we can conquer time by stuffing space.

Dionysos had set out from the Indies, so they say, dressed in brightly colored silks, laden with bracelets and rings, his eyes smeared with rouge and his nails dyed cinnabar red. He went on and on in the direction of Greece, and as he approached her clear graceful shores, he cast off his clothes one by one, threw his bangles into the sea, and stopped dying and smearing himself. When at last he reached the Gulf of Eleusis and set foot on the sacred shore, he was stark naked. The god of drunkenness had become the god of beauty. Such is also the path of art.

■ SALAMANCA

■ EMPTY IS THE GREAT flagstone courtyard of the
University. Some three centuries ago, thousands of students
had thronged here, like ants, from all over the world. Uproar;
discussions; life; movement; what agitation used to stir
in this wasp's nest of wisdom! Students who were boozers
and libertines, or pale mystics, moved back and forth in
their motley costumes. Some belonged to the military
orders of Saint Jacob. On their chests they wore a red
cross in the shape of a sword hilt. Others dressed in green
or blue or yellow capes; others in black or snow-white cassocks—all treading the flagstones in the courtyard, making
signs in the dark corridors, hanging out the windows. They
used to hold discussions on Aristotelian syllogisms; or Scot's
and Thomas Aquinas' theology; or the unmoved center of the
Universe: the earth. These students were democratically
organized and chose their professors on their own. All day
long they discussed and pursued theology; then at night took
to wine, song, women or prayer.

Nowadays: peace and solitude, a heavenly felicity. Autumnal sun—the grass twined pleasantly over the stones, doing its best to uproot them; a white cat sitting on the doorstep, sunning itself. All the hubbub has faded away. The
metaphysical problems that had once stirred the air—whence
we have come and whither we are going—have not been
solved. They have only vanished, and in their place have come

the silent grass and the cat sunning itself. The futile delirium that constitutes both the nobility and torment of man is now past. I recalled the brave lads in our popular ballad, who built a fortress to save themselves from Death. And Death stepped forward and blew lightly: "There was a slight upheaval, and the fortress was no longer there."

Over in a corner of the courtyard, a sad sunlight fell gently on the statue of the likable, most genial monk, Luis Ponce de León, the great sixteenth-century lyric poet and wise professor of theology. A fanatic champion for the popular tongue, he proclaimed to "infinite and grief-filled Spain," that if we want the people to become enlightened and saved, we must write in their own language. Only by using the language of the people could we resurrect ancient wisdom as well. "Thus both wise men and men devoid of wisdom," preached the enlightened monk, "will come out for the better."

As was only natural, he was imprisoned. For five years he suffered tortures in prison without complaining, consoled by the idea that, like the first Christians, he too was a martyr for the truth. Then later, with his gift for expressing his grief rhythmically and making it into verse, he found relief. Art wrought its miracle again. Through his verse the imprisoned poet opened the locked doors. And as a free man, he sang the praises of heaven and earth, with tenderness and melancholy. Grace, ineffable sweetness, modest pride, nobility, a serene rapture to lyrical heaven:

> *Here their envy and lies*
> *locked me behind the gate;*
> *yet glad the humble state*
> *of him, withdrawn and wise,*
> *far from the evil world*

> *in this delightful field,*
> *spending his life alone*
> *with modest room and board,*
> *with God his sole reward,*
> *and jealousy unknown.**

After five years they let him out of prison. Calmly he started back for this same University of Salamanca, climbed into his old post and began his lessons again with his usual simple phrase, as though he'd interrupted his class but yesterday: *"Decíamos ayer* . . . As we were saying yesterday . . ."

In the deserted courtyard an old woman emerged, her hands full of corn. She began to call her chickens hoarsely: *"Pollo! Pollo! Pollo!"* A red rooster came out and, behind it, some ten well-fed chickens. Suddenly in the space around Luis Ponce de León's feet, life stirred, humble and eternal.

All day long I wandered through the narrow little streets of this fallen academe of Salamanca. The old bitter questions buzzed around my ears like wasps. It seems the very air here is haunted, as though the fiery and loquacious Don Quixotes of wisdom hadn't quite rotted away beneath the turf. Inside myself I was reliving time and I could see how impulsively the spirit had stridden over the land and rocks of Spain. For the first time I was aware how the Pyrenees severed Europe from Africa. The Renaissance, by uniting the ancient Greek and Christian minds, opened up new sources of joy and creation in the vitals of human beings, but beyond the Pyrenees the Renaissance never spread. For the passionate Spain we know from the *Romances*, and the Gothic arch and Arabian melody remained a virgin.

The Renaissance, born in Italy, offspring of the illicit

---

* Translated by Willis Barnstone.

marriage between Apollo and the Virgin, crossed the borders and entered France, taking her by storm. The deep-rooted native French Renaissance, which had begun with the troubadours and the superb Gothic churches, was suddenly interrupted. It took a wrong turn and rejected all that was most fervently its own. The heroic souls born on her own soil were left to die, without being immortalized. The gates of Paris opened and the ancient Greeks entered, with their chitons and helmets, their myths and their gods, and the whole motley joyful band of the tragic Dionysos. A moment of fatal misunderstanding and madness. The divine fruit that had begun to grow on the Gothic tree withered. In Spain, however, these ancient monsters, the Achaeans and Romans, could not cross the borders for long. The Holy Inquisition—may it rest in peace!—had lit the pyres, and the ancient monsters were prevented from coming any closer. A few did cross the borders secretly and did manage to enter the homes and theaters and climb onto the stage. But the mass of the people remained faithful to their own forefathers and jeered at the newcomers as charlatans from the moment they appeared.

That is why, at its high point, Spanish poetry preserved its unique consistency. Playing on their lyres, the common people sang of their own heroes, their central hero being the Cid. Their theater, based on the *Romances*, unconcerned with the classical unities, flourished in close contact with the Spanish soil. They worshiped heroism and thirsted for adventure and had a violent lust for life and amorous exploits. Spanish knights, Spanish laughter, Spanish tears. The poet feels his feet riveted deep in the earth of Spain, and this gives him joy. A contemporary poet* eulogizes this age-old

---

* Pedro Salinas. Translated by Willis Barnstone.

joy felt by the artisan in standing firmly rooted, like a tree, in his own earth:

> *Earth. Nothing more.*
> *Earth. Nothing less.*
> *And let that be enough for you.*
> *For on the earth our feet are planted,*
> *on our feet the torso straight,*
> *on our torso the head firm,*
> *and there, in our forehead's refuge*
> *the pure idea, and in the pure idea*
> *tomorrow, the key*
> *—tomorrow—of eternity.*
> *Earth. No more nor less.*
> *And let that be enough for you.*

Hence we understand perfectly the exuberant joy and pride of that Titan sprung from the earth of Spain: Lope de Vega. He felt that his soul was not rootless or floating in air or a thing of the moment, isolated, destined to be lost along with his body. On the contrary, he felt in harmony with Spain—at one with her mountains and rivers and her people, both those already born and those not yet born. His temporary words were the words of all Spain, and so he could say proudly and with conviction: "I believe in one Lope de Vega, omnipotent father, poet of heaven and earth, poet of all visible and invisible things . . ."

But this joy was not long-lived. Haughty Bourbon monarchs crossed the Pyrenees, bringing with them the Greco-Roman disease. The people, with their strong unspoiled instinct, reacted. They did not want to see works like these. They could not understand them. They were not moved by them. What did they care about Andromache and Medea and Agamemnon? They rushed to Spanish works to see their own heroes, the familiar well-loved figures that had come out of their own vitals, that mirrored their own lives. Royal decrees were issued forbidding the performance of Spanish works of their golden age of poetry. The disease brought by the Bourbons withered all the flowers of native origin. Theatrical works, poems, romances were now all tailored on Parisian models. How could the exotic Spanish tree, once so full of sap, bloom now? The Spanish spirit has no connection with the Frankish. There is an abyss between them. The one is logical, balanced. Even in its most violent rage, it likes refinement. It subjects passion to a logical sober framework. It is disciplined by intellectual laws. It proclaims the intellect as the apex of human endeavor. The other spirit, the Spanish, all unbalanced, rough, agitated and explosive, scorning logic and fixed canons, acclaims passion as the sole immortal source of life and art.

Generations passed. This mental slavery weighed heavily on the Spanish spirit, prevented Spain from lifting up her head. But a strong race, even in the depths of slavery, goes on working, underground, secretly, ripening the moment for her own deliverance. So after a time, its deliverer is born: a hero or a saint, or sometimes a combination of both.

So after many generations, Spain did produce her own deliverer: a saint, a calm, enormously mild man who taught Philosophy of Law at the University of Madrid. Don Francisco Jiner de los Rios was delicate, a man of few words and so meticulous that he couldn't bear even a scrap of paper on the floor, as one of his students told me. He always wore a white tie. His conversation was full of irony, humor, warm vigor. Such was the physical instrument chosen by the spirit of the Spanish revival to take charge and lead the attack. He was not like the other Spanish heroes we know so well, with their thundering voices and powerful bodies and fiery lusts. For Spain has a rich character, capable of all extremes.

Without fierce cries or vulgar proclamations, calmly, by his teaching and life, Don Francisco had begun the struggle. He founded the "Free School of Education," the alma mater of present-day Spain. His aim was to create new human beings, men and women alike; to cultivate not only their mind, but their heart and soul as well. Like all genuine Spaniards, Don Francisco had little love for any one-sided cultivation of the mind. He regarded this as dangerous, debasing to the human being. His purpose was to create perfect human beings, who would be tightly integrated in thought, in feeling and in action.

Such a school was a genuine and unexpected miracle in the Spain of that time, with all her priest-ridden schools. Joy, an exile from all those unsmiling, narrow-minded, moldy, professorial brains, found refuge here in his cradle of freedom. Don Francisco's pupils laughed and played, took excursions, went swimming. And by the time they had grown up, they had created another Spain inside themselves, utterly different from the Spain around them. The war began between the two Spains: the ideated and the actual. As always, at first the actual Spain was winning—with her organization, her kings, her army, her priests, her uneducated masses. But as always, the Idea, wounded and tearful, was slowly progressing. The more they tortured and hunted it, the more courageous it grew and the more it progressed. "The scent of the lotus," says an Indian proverb, "travels in harmony with the wind. The scent of holiness travels against the wind." Pre-eminently, against the wind. For apparently, the Good, in order to become firmly rooted in the human soul, must struggle and shed its blood; must have an enemy, day and night, compelling it to stay awake and not give in to the natural tendency of evil in the world. Willy-nilly, this enemy works with the Good and also pushes men upward. Woe betide us if cruelty, arrogance, injustice perish from the earth!

Don Francisco carried on the struggle calmly and persistently, with a smile. The "scent of holiness" spread from one end of Spain to the other. Any spirit touched by it was metamorphosed, and in turn that spirit, according to its own grace, metamorphosed the "scent," made it into a heroic call to arms, an outburst of anger or a cry of protest. Students, with characters utterly different from the professor's, sprang forward from all the corners of Spain. Don Francisco was delighted. He knew this was a fine sign. For when an idea is capable of leading so many different spirits, obviously it must be greater than the brain that crystallized it. Obviously the desire must be wider than the individual, must be deeply rooted in the needs of the masses and the age.

Don Francisco felt he had fulfilled his destiny. An old man now, he crossed his hands and died. He disappeared noiselessly as evening light. One of his students, the poet Antonio Machado, described his departure with great feeling:

> When my master went away
> this morning's light
> told me: My brother Francisco
> has not worked for three days.
> Did he die? We only know
> he left along a bright path,
> telling us: Give me
> a mourning of works and hopes.
> Be good and no more. Be what I have been
> among you: a soul.

Be alive, life goes on,
the dead die and shadows pass;
he who gives receives; he who has lived is living.
Let anvils boom and church bells be still!

To find another, purer light
our brother—the happy old man who led
a saintly life—has left
the light of dawn, the sun in shops.
Oh yes, friends, carry
his body to the mountains,
to the blue summits
of broad Guadarrama!
There are the sunken gulches
of green pines and singing wind.
His heart is at peace
below a chaste holm oak,
in thyme fields of playful
yellow butterflies.
There one day our master
dreamt of a new blossoming in Spain.*

* Translated by Willis Barnstone.

■ AVILA

■ Dry, deserted, stiff-necked is this towering workshop where the Spanish spirit was tempered. Central Castile: low hovels in which the people and the animals eat and sleep together; freezing winds; tall bony shepherds with huge fiery eyes; shepherd boys, baked in the sun, coming and going among the rocks, as they follow their famished goats. . . .

The genuine Spaniard still has inside him a deep nostalgia for the nomadic life. He scorns the peasants bent over to cultivate the soil. When he was able to keep Arab slaves, he used to entrust to them the cultivation of his land. The Spaniard, during these eras of his glory, pursued his real profession: he fought battles, traveled, roamed and wandered like a vagabond in the New World—not to preach the religion of Christ or to grab gold, the almighty temptress. These were only excuses; if they hadn't been there, he would have found others. He fought and wandered, because such was his nature. He longed for adventures. He struggled to escape from a mediocre life; struggled to find time to finish some great work before dying. As in Dürer's marvellous work, Death gallops on horseback behind the Spaniard, who is also galloping on horseback. Like two brave combatants, they stream on toward the grave. But before this macabre race is over, the Spaniard looks yearningly around him at the earth and sea and woman, and craves hungrily to see, touch, say farewell. . . .

So we can explain the apparently great antinomy in the Spanish spirit, which so many wise men have not been able to understand through logic: Passion and Nonentity! These are the two poles around which the Spanish spirit revolves: passion, desire, a warm embrace of life . . . and, at the same time, the awareness that all this is nothing, Nonentity, that Death is our great heir. But the more aware a strong spirit is of Nonentity, the more intensely he lives each fleeting, futile moment. For strong spirits, Death is the keenest stimulant.

In the heart of Castile on a hilltop, rises the fortress of Avila: "all stones and saints." Its ramparts are still intact, with their eighty-eight towers, their indented embrasures, and their empty subterranean porticoes. These ramparts encompass the present-day hovels, villas, churches and monasteries of the celebrated city.

More than ten centuries ago, in this square, now so desolate and silent, the Arabian workshops resounded. The dark craftsmen beat their bronze. The voice of the Moslem crier was heard calling the followers to prayer. And surely there must have been a fountain gurgling in the middle of the square, while all around—inside the closed high-walled houses, behind the lattices—impatient black eyes stared eagerly down on the street below. *Ovriaki:* shrill cries and mules with green and red trappings and wily merchants, gaudily colored rags, uproar, spice shops, hidden gardens, a melancholy xylophone playing beneath the new moon— till the wrathful Christians swept down from the north, and the dark craftsmen vanished along with their women painted in cinnabar and rouge. Now over the same narrow streets, abbots on well-fed mules began to pass, and iron-clad knights and women with locked iron chastity belts.

One day—it must have been about 1522—a knight rode into Avila. He was half laughing, half angry. There was a boy about ten years old, in tears, sitting on the rump of his horse. The knight dismounted at an old villa, grabbed the boy by the nape of the neck and set him down on the ground. A little lass, who couldn't have been more than seven, flew out to the doorstep. She caught sight of her brother, bit her lip stubbornly and angrily, but didn't breathe a word. "Teresa," the knight called to her half-angrily, as he dismounted. "It's all your fault! You set his brain on fire! You hear there—he says he wants to go to the Moors and preach the Bible! The little scamp!"

The young Teresa gave no answer, only took her brother by the hand. He was still wailing. And she whispered in his ear: "Rodrigo, aren't you ashamed of yourself to be crying? Wait till we're a bit older and we'll go together."

The young Teresa read the lives of the saints, and her imagination and heart swelled. In the rainbow-colored miniatures, she could see the Moors in their green and red turbans, cutting off the saints' heads. She saw tall white lilies growing out of the saints' blood, and she marvelled at the New Jerusalem with its emerald walls up in the blue air. "*Para siempre! . . . Siempre! . . . Siempre! . . .* For ever! . . . And ever! . . . And ever!" These, as she later confessed to us, were the words she loved to say over and over again, when she was a little girl chattering with her brother Rodrigo about flights and martyrdoms.

In this fiery atmosphere she grew up, waiting expectantly. As a young girl, even in her father's stern household, she used to daydream of heroic deeds and adventures, of escaping far away for ever and ever and ever!

They shut her in a convent. For the noblemen's daughters of the time the convent was a sort of gay school for girls, where the young nuns exchanged visits with their girl friends. They used to gossip for hours on end in the *locutorio*. They were also visited by their relatives and men friends, who used to bring them worldly gifts such as little bottles of cologne, ointments for their skin, exotic fruits from the newly discovered Indies, sweet potatoes, bananas, coffee. . . . Occasionally, they also received intricate acrostics, where heavenly and earthly love were fused with the finesse of the troubadours and the hyperbole of the romantics. So the dangerous pill of the flesh was gilded both innocently and roguishly. The upper-class convents, having all these liberties, turned into worldly gathering-places, where philosophical and artistic themes were discussed; gay light-hearted academies, where, according to the customs of the age, they conversed of Platonic love and the ideal lover. Here the young ladies lived the delicate gay life that suited them, the life that they could not live in the laughterless households of their fathers or at the macabre court of Philip II. The emissary from Venice, after seeing the blissful life lived by the young nuns, rightly commented: "The nuns in these convents are in the antechamber of Paradise." Teresa, for the first time in her life, began to laugh and play in this convent where they had shut her. She began to feel how pleasant the world can be. She felt proud of being able to speak well, of always finding the most brilliant retort to every argument. These small worldly successes gave her great joy. Her life began to roll along happily, self-contentedly, free of care.

One night Teresa's soul was shaken with horror. She suddenly sensed that she was going to her doom. Hell gaped suddenly in front of her, underneath her feet. "Let me save,

O let me save my soul!" she cried out. "I must bring the old virtue back to the monasteries."

At the same time in the same way, Don Quixote was also shaken, as he read all the lives of the knights, and he too cried out: "Let me save, O let me save my soul! I must bring the old virtue back to fallen knighthood!" Don Quixote and Saint Teresa are a pair. Theirs is the same identical outcry; they each had the same purpose: to save their souls, or rather, to offer them extravagantly, for a higher purpose.

From that night on began the heroic and often humorous adventures of the saint. In her little carriage, she rushed day and night to villages and cities to preach and enforce the new monastic rules, and to found her own model convents. People made fun of her, threatened her, made a thousand and one difficulties for her. The houses they gave her for her convents were often about to collapse. Rain leaked through the roof, and there wasn't so much as a chair or a table or a blanket. But Saint Teresa, always jolly, always full of optimism and good humor, took the houses by storm, begging for the most essential furnishings and a bit of bread and oil and wooden logs.

"Love means energy!" she liked to repeat. And for her holiness was not a state of excitement or a brave feat lasting but a moment. It was a daily labor of patience and hard work. It was no grand assault, but a day-to-day battle down in the trenches, in the dirt and mud. That was how Saint Teresa fought. She faced hunger and grumbling complaints and threats patiently, mockingly. When there was only a mouthful of bread, and the nuns started sulking, she would laugh and tell them: "It's better that way! Better! When the body's fat, the soul grows skinny."

From time to time, in those damp cold monasteries, where there was often no bread or fire or straw mattress for them to sleep on, Teresa would snatch up a baking pan, shake it like a tambourine and begin chanting and dancing in the courtyard. She would laugh at herself too, exclaiming between laughs: "O you silly brains!" The nuns, shocked and hungry, used to watch her in amazement. But then suddenly the saint would whirl around, stare at them, and utter the following unexpectedly bitter phrase: "All this I am forced to do in order to stay alive!" Also, this frequently repeated outcry, which is so genuinely Spanish: "Y *todo es nada!*" And everything is nothing!

One spring evening, in the convent courtyard in Salamanca, Saint Teresa was conversing peacefully with the nuns as they walked back and forth over the flagstones. All of a sudden a young nun sprang up in the middle of the courtyard, with a tambourine and castanets. She began to sing and dance: "Come here, come here, dear eyes! Come, my sweet Christ!"

All at once the saint felt her arms paralyzed. Her eyes closed. Her whole body froze and she fell senseless to the flagstones. The nuns, in terror, carried her to her cell. Weeping, they stretched her out on her dry mattress. When Teresa came back to her senses, she wrote her marvellous ode to God: "*Muero, porque no muero!* I die because I do not die!"

This was her first ecstasy and loss of consciousness. But she was afraid of these moments. She did not believe in them, nor did she want them. She preferred to stand firmly on the solid earth, with her soul riveted to her body. Whenever she saw one of the nuns in a state of hysteria, of falling down and writhing, she used to command angrily: "Hit her a few times till she comes back to her senses!"

For Teresa the holy life was not a mad fury that sprouts wings and tries to escape from the world. It was a patient, hard-working life of love. As with art, so with holiness: so-called "inspiration," enthusiasm, rapture, madness, even if they are divine, are suspect and diabolical elements that may lead one astray. All these murky, raw elements must be refined by the patient, utterly severe, day-to-day working of the mind. Patience, logic, gaiety, love—these are the four mares that pulled the carriage of Saint Teresa and her soul.

I pondered on this ecstatic worker, who so fruitfully and perfectly fused within herself Don Quixote and Sancho. I pondered on her walking swiftly through the deserted hilly streets of Avila. Aside from the peculiar characteristics given her by her own epoch, I was trying to see, beneath her nun's habit, the flame that was hers, naked and solid.

In order to enjoy intensely the fleeting moment, there always has been and always will be but one system. For this system summons and commands all our forces: viz., we must follow a rhythm that is higher than ourselves. Only in this way can man's existence become noble and integrated. Only thus can his energy transcend the stifling limits of the individual. Only he who believes and obeys such a rhythm can live perfectly his own tiny individual life. As soon as a believer climbs onto the pyre or sets about doing a brave deed or even just sits calmly on his own doorstep, the life inside him erupts, all flooded with light. In the flicker of an eyelash, he feels such joy as all the logical non-believers cannot feel in a whole century. The faithful, most ascetic method has always been the surest and most fruitful for man's living intensely—not the life to be hereafter—but the present life here and now on earth. Only through faith can the masses be elevated. What do we mean by their being "elevated"? We mean the subjection of their desires and needs to a hyperindividual, or rather, to the deepest human rhythm.

Our duty, if we find this rhythm, is to ally ourselves with it. And how? By following its own method: viz., by transmuting as much material substance as possible into Spirit. In the human realm, this struggle is complex and uncertain. For what we call "material substance" and what we call "Spirit" are interchangeable. Whatever was once a movement or an impulse upward in the foregoing generation—whatever was once Spirit—becomes, in the subsequent generation, motionless, stifled, heavy, and in time reacts just like substance. A Breath (call it Religion, Race, Ideal, Fatherland) that had once risen like fire, that had once created, dies down after a few centuries; it is slowly reduced to embers, and finally becomes a hindrance to any new upsurging Breath. Finally, after it in turn has exhausted its power in all possible forms of work, it too peters out, dies down and at the very center of the struggle becomes an obstacle.

This rhythm, which is as old as time, older than man, has dominated human history. A mass rises up full of desires and needs. It gains power, both spiritual and material. It establishes its own laws. It creates civilizations and then, little by little, settles down into a self-satisfied stagnation. Another mass of people rises up with energy, because they are hungry; or because a new god is marshaling them; or because they are the victims of injustice and want to introduce justice. However, all these excuses, which are genuine, always conceal the main reason: They rise up, because they feel that they are slaves, or even more precisely: because there is Someone inside them who is a slave struggling to get free.

Some Breath, independent of human will, moves the masses in every age and, by using man as a tool, creates what we call "Civilization." Or else it annihilates the works and ideas of the tired old civilization. There is a rhythm that excites men's spirits and forces them to dance as it wants: in a balanced calm way or with the vertiginous speed of catastrophe. What people often call the "Spirit of the Age," over-hastily and superficially, is actually a demon— something higher than man. It rides an era or a race like a beast of burden, spurring it on to do deeds beyond its own capacities, beyond any logical anticipation or any immediate necessity. At these grand moments, all people—good or bad, enemies or friends, willing or not—cooperate with this demon. They are all carried away by its rhythm: either they understand and abet the rhythm, or they react against it and so force the corresponding party to organize and multiply.

As I left Avila, I bid farewell to Saint Teresa. In another age, under other circumstances, the same fire would have had another face, would have danced another dance in the air. On a Greek island in pre-Socratic times, during the heavenly springtime, with amorous and happy young schoolgirls all around her, her name would have been Sappho. And she would have sung odes to the same god under another name. If she had lived in our own time, plunged in the heavy modern reality, she would have seen injustice and hunger and pain. Bereft of the old god, who had given men something to grip, who had left reward and punishment to the afterlife, she would have embarked on another kind of crusade. Surrounded by other fiery spirits, she would have taken another path.

The identically same spirit and fire go by different names, according to the needs of each age and the ingredients of each race. But the practiced eye is not deceived.

■ THE ESCORIAL

■ W~HILE THE PAGANS~ were roasting Saint Lawrence on the torture rack, the saint turned around to his cooks and remarked, with unexpected humor: "I'm well roasted on one side. Turn me over on the other side now!"

There is a little church in honor of this saint, wedged in among the precipitous rocks of the Escorial, 60 kilometers northwest of Madrid. Philip II had vowed that if he was victorious in battle, he would build a great monastery and dedicate it to Saint Lawrence. He was victorious, and in 1563 he began to carry out his vow. The pale fanatic king wanted to construct a house for his soul—a sheath to hold his cold strange brain. He cared nothing for the beauties and joys of this world. He refused to soothe his agony with curves and superfluous designs and bagatelles, such as please the carnal eye. He wished to carve in granite a fierce cave for his soul to burrow away.

He hired the best master-masons—Juan Battista of Toledo first, and then the marvellous Juan Herrera—and ordered them to build him a gigantic monastery in the shape of a torture rack, since he was going to dedicate it to Saint Lawrence. The construction took more than twenty years. Philip supervised it in person, keeping a sleepless watch, seated on a throne they had carved for him high up on the rock. With his steel blue frozen gaze, he watched and watched as it rose slowly, slowly amid the wild cliffs: his cell, his palace, and his tomb all in one. Like a silkworm, this silent, jaundiced king was weaving his own cocoon, patiently and tremblingly.

Would his soul be saved? Would it one day awake and bore through the gray stone walls, and fly like a yellow butterfly up over the enormous flower of God? Dressed in his black velvet costume, Philip, mute and grief-worn, and possessed by ominous divinations, sat on his chiseled rock watching his tomb rise higher and higher. It was an enormous tomb: 208 meters long, 162 wide, with 1100 outside windows, 1600 inside, 1200 doors, 86 staircases, and 16 courtyards. The surface of this giant torture rack was the royal palace, and the feet of the rack were formed by the four towers, each one 56 meters high. With his merciless gaze, Philip watched and watched the green and yellow blocks of granite joined and sealed, fitting out his final place of refuge. Ill and pallid-lipped, he went on watching in despair. What was the secret of this great king who never smiled?

Today as I was crossing the great courtyard of the Escorial, recollecting the fate of this tragic Othello of the Church, I suddenly remembered an old biography of one of the saints: Saint John the Faster was on his deathbed, in his hermit's cell in the desert. Off on the other side of the desert, Saint Nile learned the black tidings from an angel. He rose, took up his stick, but, owing to his great old age, he could not move. His disciples lifted him onto a stretcher, and so they carried him wrapped in his rags and all rolled up like a ball to his friend the hermit, who was in the pangs of death. "Quickly! Quickly!" Nile cried out along the way, thumping his stick. "Quickly! I must get to him while he's still alive!" But he did not get to him in time. The hermit had already died. Nile bent over to give him the last embrace. And then—lo! a miracle! says the biography—Saint John raised himself slightly and whispered something in Nile's ear, then straightway fell back again, dead.

In terror, Nile's disciples rushed over to kiss the hands and feet of their Master. They asked him: "What did he tell you? What did he tell you? Your eyes are dazed with horror, Holy Father!" But Nile did not want to confess anything. He never told the secret to any man. His life did not change in any way. Only from that time on, his lips never smiled again.

And today in the Escorial, suddenly a satanic thought tore through my mind and made it all as clear as day. I knew what the hermit had told him. I had found the secret! Saint John the Faster had murmured into the ear of his friend and companion in agony: "Brother, we are doomed! There is no Paradise!"

A Spaniard could bear this terrible revelation and go on living unperturbed, as if he had heard nothing; as if he could still hope; as if he were not certain of his doom. Philip, however, was a Hapsburg and he had not heard anything. Perhaps only in this icy piercing air of the Sierra Guadarrama could he sense these bitter forebodings. And that is why he was no longer able to laugh.

Amid these bloodcurdling fantasies, I was climbing the staircases of the Escorial. In the magnificent marble sub-terranean passages, I touched the tombs of the Spanish kings. The last tomb was still open, lying in wait for Alfonso XIII, the lantern-jawed king, whose carefree travels and jaunts between Fontainebleau and Prague, between Prague and the Indies, were all in vain. His marble tomb here in the Escorial lies wide open like a hungry mouth, and this living morsel, in spite of all his present comings and goings, cannot escape it.

This thick-jawed king was no worse than his ancestors. In many ways he was better. But he fell a victim—and very rightly so!—to ancestral sins. His ancestors ate the sour grapes, and he suffered the ill effects. Such are the dictates of deeper justice. In time and place, the members of a family or of a race are mutually responsible. They are tightly bound, and constitute a self-contained, unified organism. In the person of the ancestor, the grandchild also sins, and in the person of the grandchild, the ancestor is punished. The original sin of the Bible has a deep significance, both symbolical and physiological.

Autumn. In the gardens of the Escorial, the chestnut trees glowed, all golden. There were yellow leaves piled up on the ground. They glistened on the damp earth like freshly minted gold florins. The sun came out, and the gray monastery lit up and seemed to smile for a moment. In the main courtyard, the children of the Escorial School were playing. The whole imperial edifice had come to life, like a cypress tree in the evening light when flocks of swallows sit perched on it. Several priests, who were teachers here, moved to and fro, conversing and gesticulating. With their black cassocks, their octagonal black hats and silk tassels and their clean-shaven, wrinkled faces, they came and went in the sunlight, swiftly like hunted blackbirds.

I went on into the courtyard and mingled with the children. I was scrutinizing them one by one, trying to guess their fate. How would they be when they emerged from the monkish hands? How many of these gay, dark-eyed Spanish lads would be saved? A generation ago now, another child was playing in this same courtyard in the same way. He was a laconic, stubborn boy, who loved judiciously chosen clear words, self-possession, order. "In this rough army barracks," he himself tells us, "I learned to cultivate my own ego, and not to base any hope on sympathy. Inside myself,

I did not feel the spirit of sacrifice or humility. Nor did I find relief in tears. . . ."

Gradually his character took on the rigid virtues of the grim monastery: the will power and discipline; the obedience in all details to a central idea. No frivolity, no yielding to fortuitous or imaginary elements. Equal rigid lines; an unembellished style; strength devoid of grace. "The Escorial," he writes elsewhere, "is unapproachable, almost superhuman. It is friendly to no man. The truth expressed in it can never be congenial with irony."

I was thinking of Manuel Azaña as I gazed at these little Spanish children, one by one. For a moment they had slipped out of the priests' hands to play. Which of these youths would have the luck to find the historical moment congenial with himself, that would enable all the buds inside him to bear fruit? Which of them would find—or create—the historical moment?

The success or failure of a human being is something utterly mysterious. Numberless indeterminate factors, both external to man and intrinsic in him, contribute. Often what he himself is worth does not play the main role. Azaña himself admits to us that all his life he spent walking alone through the streets of Madrid, by day in winter, by night in the summertime. He used to go to the café and talk for hours on end with his few friends. Silent, hands in pockets, he used to wander around the big rooms of the athenaeum. He wrote a few small pamphlets that passed by without notice. He'd already turned fifty and had done nothing. He was a lost case.

Then one day, as he describes it, he went to the Escorial to see his old school, to learn whether his old teachers were still alive. He entered the courtyard with fluttering heart. In the far corner of the courtyard, he saw an old monk sitting in the sun. It was Don Mariano, his beloved teacher. They began talking of past times, and as they recalled them, they felt both stirred and hilarious.

"And what are you doing?" his old teacher asked him.

"I walk around Madrid, up and down. At home I smoke."

"You always were lazy. Is there nothing that interests you?"

"My love of life is stronger and nobler the more my brain mellows. But I am just tormenting myself. I am forcing myself to cast salt on the fruitful earth."

"Your words make me sad. You are more blinded than ever by vanity."

"On my lips, I feel the essence of ashes."

"Do you have peace of mind?"

"Almost always."

"That is the worst of all."

"I am not dead, Father Mariano! My peace springs from my experience."

"Experience must be tamed. If you had struggled with the angel, you would have been saved."

"From the hour I was born, there has been a mysterious invisible companion accompanying me. This companion does not seem to be an angel. It is constantly displeased with me, as though I might be capable of creating another, better life. And it never tells me who it is and what it wants. I would be delighted to kill it, but I am unable to. I kick it with my foot, but it just comes back again. It is a real monster."

"May God grant you one day to hear what this monster is saying to you and so, one day, may you become our Prodigal Son!"

This is what Azaña wrote in 1927, a revealing dialogue, rife with bitterness and guilty conscience. Azaña's soul was aware that his life was being wasted. At the same time, he was filled with violent undefined desires, devoid of hope. The "monster" (or real Azaña) scornfully, angrily observed the other (the superficial Azaña) frittering away his time in the streets, rolling around the cafés. After several years, the "monster" was destined to assume flesh and become visible.

As I left the children at their peaceful play, I said to myself: "May God (that is to say, Necessity and Coincidence) grant that many of these young men become staunch revolutionaries and others of them fanatic conservatives. So it will be possible for both camps to organize themselves with faith, and so the battle can explode with all possible ferocity."

I approached the priest-teachers, who were walking in the courtyard, their cassocks waving in the wind like wings. How the "turnings of the cycle" change, up and down, up and down. Here were the offspring of the Holy Inquisition, who had once held and crushed Spain in the palms of their hands. Now they are squeezed into a few monasteries. They are thrown out of their splendid palaces. Their greatest power is taken from them: the souls of the children.

"Are the children your pupils?" I asked, playing the ignoramus.

"Yes, of course, *caballero*. They're our pupils."

"But I thought a law had been passed . . ."

"It will never be passed!" a tall, bony, pock-marked monk retorted angrily and shrilly.

How I liked him! Like the saints of Ribera. In his eyes blazed all the pyres of the Holy Inquisition. Ah! Would that a new band of Moors might swoop down on faithless Spain again—merciless, dark, fiery, killing bodies in order to save souls! Here in Spain, it is impossible to dislike a man, no matter what he says, no matter what he does. The Spaniards have such a violent, unquenchable fire in their eyes that, in their presence, all differences and ideologies vanish. What an insignificant thing: the "Idea," in the presence of the black, mad Spanish eyes. Once again, I understood that the thing that counts is not the *what*, but the *how*. Only this deserves consideration. I had always had my own mental image of my own Paradise and my own Hell. They were utterly different from the officially recognized Paradise and Hell. All the "warm" people, whether virtuous or villainous, would enter my Paradise. All the "cold" people, whether virtuous or villainous, would enter my Hell. And at the very bottom of Hell would be the cold virtuous people!

I stared closely at these Catholic priests in the evening sun of the Escorial. I shook their hands vigorously as I said goodbye to them. Their kind faces were stamped indelibly in my mind: all of them would enter my Paradise.

The late afternoon gilded the granite rocks. The light limped from rock to rock like a wounded bird on its way upward. For a moment, it rested on the peak of the opposite mountain, seemed to pirouette upward, then disappeared. The mute murmur of evening, like the tigress' melody, enveloped the monastery. And the giant torture rack of the Escorial faded into darkness.

■ MADRID

■ GAY, WARM-HEARTED oasis atop a harsh barren plateau. The highest in altitude of any European capital: the nearest heaven. The Andalusians rightly say: "The throne of the Spanish king is the first after the throne of God."

In the heart of the inhuman arid land of New Castile, the obstinate Royal prerogative pitched this noisy colorful tent: a real miracle of the desert. Travel on foot over the ground between Avila and Madrid, in order to appreciate this miracle. It is like the amazement felt after walking for days in the Sinai desert, in the midst of the barren mountain ranges and steaming sands, and then suddenly coming across the superb garden with its olive and almond and orange trees flanking the famous monastery. It seems a mirage. And after all, what else is the human will in the infinite horror of time and place? Is it not a mirage lasting but a moment—several centuries—set between two fatal icebergs? At times the mirage fades. At times it flares up again, and so on until the earth will be catapulted back into the flames.

Similarly, in this desert of Castile, with its yellow and red earth and its ash-green granite, the joy of suddenly coming on Madrid is even greater. For as well as joy, there is a feeling of pride in the will and tenacity of man.

Madrid is truly a moral triumph, heightening man's belief in his own virtue. And when I say "virtue," I mean tenacity and strength. That is why straight off, from the first moment, Madrid arouses sympathy, as a landmark of human triumph.

Stand for a moment on a height and admire her. Put your hand to your ear like a megaphone and listen to her: church bells, people, hubbub, train whistles, thousands of indistinct voices, the dark rustle of a beehive. In the sunlight Madrid, stretched out along the narrow banks of the Manzanares, looks like the naked Maja, that diabolical whirly nude painted by Goya. Her loins glisten. Her curves undulate. She smiles slyly, like an earthly jade reclining on the blue pillow of heaven. The sun rises and sets over her. The moon passes and is caught in her curves. The rains and icy mountain winds come. The warm sunny weather returns, and she continues smiling, calmly, seductively, sprawling in the desert.

At her feet, like an out-of-breath and parched lover, the Manzanares River gasps and pants. How many people have vented their malice in mockery of it! "Dried-up old well!" Góngora called it, and queried:

"What ails you, Manzanares? Why are you so dry?"

"A donkey passed by yesterday and drank me all up," was the poor river's answer.

Lope de Vega accused it of "being thirsty and drinking its own water." And the great Spanish writer, Quevedo: "Ah, just one drop of water, for my mosquitoes and frogs are dying of thirst!" When Philip II built a magnificent bridge over it, someone remarked: "Now let's sell the bridge to buy some water!" And someone else said: "Philip has made the bridge. His heir apparent will have to make the river!" The only kind word about it came from an ambassador sent by the German Emperor Rudolph II: "It is the kindest river in Europe. One crosses it on horseback or by carriage, and it does not lose its temper!"

However, there was one deaf old man: the misanthropic

Goya, who used to stare at it from his window in the "Villa of the Deafman," admiring its abandoned state and its dusty trees. He delighted in watching the washerwomen there with their powerfully built bare legs standing in its occasional muddy puddle of water. This tragicomic "streamlet with pretensions to being a river," this Don Quixote of rivers, may have helped the despairing, isolated genius of Goya to paint the walls of his villa with those mysterious "black frescoes"—those dark primitive dreams, nightmares of the man wide awake, the toothless old man eating, the other old man, the deaf one, leaning on his stick, and behind him a monstrous companion (perhaps Death, yes, surely Death) whose mouth gapes wide open, shouting in his ear. Or the aged Cronos, that goggle-eyed dragon, holding in his huge hands his own little child and eating it. This painting, for all its horror, Goya kept in his dining room to admire while he was eating.

Secret and unceasing is the creator's collaboration with everything he sees around him every day. I like to imagine the comic Manzanares, so trampled on by clever wits, as Goya's faithful collaborator, his last friend in his final heaviest days.

Until the middle of the eighteenth century, the pigs roamed loose from house to house. The garbage was piled high on the streets. The stench was so strong that people fainted from it and, says a diarist of the period, the air was so filthy that "it soiled the gold stripes and embroidery on people's clothes."

Nowadays the heart of Madrid is an American skyscraper. But all around the large arteries branch out the poor little capillaries: peaceful lanes, lattice windows, kindly little donkeys laden with fruits, old witches with thick warts, laughing black-eyed girls with downy skin. A blind man sitting on bended knees on the ground, playing a fife and singing a wild, hoarse tune and wearing a red shawl with long tassels.

Crowds of dwarfs, lame men, one-armed cripples; others stretched out on the pavements display their horrible wounds. As the Spaniards pass by, they look at them without shuddering. Bloodshed, wounds, horror seem to be an old familiar sight for them. They feel moved by them in a calm tender way, as when they see the wounds of the saints or the blood of Christ or the blood of the bull at the sacred bull-fights. . . .

I entered a church that was all flooded with light. The crucified Christ had been set in a corner. His body dangled heavily. There was blood everywhere, huge red holes gaping in his hands and feet and ribs. Bent over, silent, covering their hair with white scarves, the women were kissing the wooden body and scarlet wounds in mad ecstasy. They went away and others came, sighing incessantly and beating their breasts. I went out into the streets to get a breath of fresh air. The sun had changed position. There were masses of clouds in the sky, and the air had turned cool, with the terrifying blue shade of the abyss. In this light the people, moving up and down like waves along the big streets, looked pale and sunk in some distant dangerous atmosphere. The women looked more lovely, and seemed to beckon that they would soon be dead.

Nowhere else do you come across women with such passionate expressions; such satanic undulations of their loins; such pure and, at the same time, animal-like femininity. You feel that all these bodies are eager to burn, with blissfully closed eyes, on the pyre of the Unholy Inquisition of carnal love. And yet the male, that superficial strutting cock, is quite mistaken! You see the Spanish women—painted like African masks, with hook-shaped curls on their temples and narrow foreheads—walking in the streets with their fatal swaying motions, their dark skin lit by metallic reflections, and olive-black eyes that stare at you indescribably, insistently luring you on. But all that is a trap, an affectation, a seductive trick, to catch—not a man, but a husband; not carnal love, but marriage. If the hearts of all the Spanish women were opened, you would find neither erotic scenes nor coy games therein. You would not even find a man. In all their hearts would be a cradle and inside the cradle, a baby. The Spanish woman is not a mistress or a companion or a slave or a plaything. She is not even a wife. She is a mother. Hers is a strong primitive race that has not yet distorted marriage into carnal love and love into a game.

In a country where the men were ever ready to lose their heads over an idea or a feeling or a gaudy utopia, the women represented those useful solid virtues of logic and balance. The Spanish woman is the solid, simple common mind that is not subject to fits of madness, that holds the keys to everyday life, locking and unlocking everyday reality. She is the precious ballast in the storm-tossed airship of the family and the nation. She leaves her husband to daydream idly of adventures and gold and glory, or to rush off on mad distant safaris. She herself never folds her arms or loses her head. She takes care of the home and raises the children and kneels in front of the bloodstained Christ, with her shopping in her hands. Calm and sure, she walks with both feet firmly on the ground. Even the most mystical of Spanish women, Saint Teresa, never lost the sacred mean. And if there is a Paradise, and if they tackle housekeeping up there too, and if there are things up there too that need locking up, surely Saint Teresa, the Spanish woman, will keep the keys.

In many popular ballads this primitive cry is clearly audible. Man, the eternal blatherer, holds his lyre and sings beneath the window in Andalusia:

"Ah, to kiss and to embrace . . ."

The woman behind the lattice window answers:

"Yes, yes; but how sparkling is the ring upon a woman's finger!"

Man, the eternal blatherer, begins again:

"Ah the moon, and the trilling nightingale, and the sweet delight of spring!"

And the woman, calm behind her lattice, repeats:

"Yes, yes; but how sparkling is the ring upon a woman's finger!"

Days of Madrid, full of noise and black eyes and women's curls and sun and rain and fertile conversations in offices and homes and museums. How the human mind delights in hearing one side, then the other side, in order to acknowledge the relative excellence of all sides; and, out of all the fanatical conflicting ideas, to try and create a single solid synthesis! Men of energy are always, of necessity, one-sided and narrow-minded. If they were otherwise, they would end up ridiculous amateurish types, incapable of hewing a definite line for their practical lives to follow, incapable of assuming responsibility. The theoretical mind, far removed from action, is very fortunate, for it has the privilege of looking both right and left, and so joining the two wings that raise the Spirit.

Spain is passing through a critical historical moment, rife with disorder, experimentalism and agony. Since 1898, the terrible year when the Spanish fleet was destroyed in Cuba, Spain has had to retreat into her shell, vanquished, exhausted, deprived of her colonies. Having lost everything except her honor, she has been forced back into the Iberian peninsula, just as Don Quixote, we remember, went back to his tower, with broken bones and ready to die.

The great lyric poet of Spain, Juan Ramón Jiménez, was saying to me yesterday:

"The catastrophe of '98 catalyzed all the powers and merits of the Spanish spirit. It was a mighty blow. The pride of our race was shaken and hurt. The so-called 'generation of '98' has this main characteristic: its thirst to learn and cross new frontiers, to see what is going on in the rest of the world. It is thirsty and hungry, after two centuries of fasting. This is how our new Renaissance began."

Admiral Cervera knew for a certainty that if he moved out of the harbor, he would be going to inevitable catastrophe. Nevertheless, he did move out, in order to preserve the supreme virtue that moves the Castilian spirit: *la honra,* honor!

The ports of Spain flooded with sick, wounded soldiers and sailors. Soon all these human wrecks scattered to the villages and cities and began to tell stories of the endless days and nights, of their disgrace and ruin. The people listened. They wept and cursed. But then they just bowed their heads again fatalistically.

However, a few intellectuals did spring up decisively. At first there were only a few, but little by little their numbers increased. They formed a circle around Don Quixote on his deathbed and began to give advice on how to save him. Each doctor had his own brand of medical wisdom. One of the attending doctors said:

"There is only one cure: religion. Only Catholicism can save Spain. So long as our country had her faith, she was great. When she lost her faith in God, she began to collapse. So back to Catholicism! Let the pyres of the Holy Inquisition be rekindled! Let all heretical books be burned and all sarcastic mouths be closed!"

"No!" the next doctor opines. "The cause of the ill lies elsewhere. It is not a question of religion, but of economics. Spain, instead of squandering her money on grandiloquent foreign adventures, should use the money for internal reconstruction; for her people, who are hungry; for her arid soil. Then Spain would still be strong and glorious."

Another answers: "It is not lack of faith or squandered money that is the root of the ill. It is ignorance. We must enlighten the people. We must open modernized schools. We must uproot illiteracy."

"All this is useless," declares another doctor, "so long as we lack freedom. Nowadays, only freedom can make nations capable of great deeds. From the cursed era when the Holy Inquisition started enslaving our spirits, Spain's downfall began. Political, social, intellectual freedom—here lies the road for salvation!"

"No!" shouts another. "Not a bit of it! All these are European ideals that are fatal for Spain! We must withdraw into our own selves. We must remain faithful to Spanish tradition. We must build our own idiosyncratic national life based on Spanish character! Here lies our salvation!"

"Not at all!" protests yet another. "Europe, European civilization, the luminaries of her science—that is our only salvation! Spain is backward and medieval and she must be Europeanized, modernized. There is no other way!"

So immediately after 1898, the various intellectual leaders of Spain began their examination—of the patient, Spain; of the Spanish spirit; of themselves. What was the cause of their collapse? What was their true historical mission? What were their weaknesses and their good qualities, and how could they be saved?

Of all the doctors surrounding the patient, Don Quixote, there were four pre-eminent ones, four great Spaniards, who opened the four main roads along which the Spanish destiny was to be directed: Joachim Costa, Angelo Ganivet, Don Miguel de Unamuno, and the then young philosopher, Ortega y Gasset. Around them fought and helped the intellectual elite of the generation: Antonio Machado, Valle-Inclán, Azorín, Pío Baroja, Miró. . . .

Joachim Costa was a notary public, but he had a voracious, inquisitive mind. He immersed himself in the most diverse studies. The Spaniards dislike specialization. They hate to confine their restless and inquisitive spirit to a single limited field. Slavish devotion to detail seems to them debasing to the human soul. Costa, the "Lion of Aragon," as he was called, plunged hungrily into tremendously diverse studies: into pre-history, sociology, folk-history, the agricultural problem, philosophy, and finally politics.

As usual in periods of renaissance, the mind had an uncontrollable desire to grasp as much as possible; to traverse the widest possible circle in theory and in action. Human beings, in these springtime eras, feel a childlike impatience. They struggle in a chaos that is fruitful and occasionally pierced by flashes of genius.

So this fiery Aragonese began to preach with the fanaticism of a prophet—writing books, writing in the newspapers, giving speeches. "Spain is lost," he cried, "so long as her eyes are turned back on her ancient grandeur, on her glorious ancestors." By doing so, she just explodes and exhausts herself in words. Shouting, orating, she believes she has fulfilled her destiny, and so folds her arms with an easy conscience. "Let us leave our ancestors behind us," proclaims the apostolic Costa, "and let us look ahead to our own contemporary needs. Let us lock and double-lock the tomb of the Cid!"

This outcry reverberated extraordinarily throughout Spain. The old guard was overwhelmed with righteous indignation: "Costa is a traitor! He is insulting the sacrosanct and holy things of Spain! He has blasphemed our greatest national hero!" But fearlessly, Costa went on preaching: "Castile saw the Cid take arms against the Moors. And then one day, Castile saw our forces coming back defeated, carrying the corpse of the Cid. Castile became Spain. Then one day she saw Columbus launch out for the West in three caravels. Another day, Spain saw our armies and fleets coming back defeated, hunted out of all our colonies, carrying the corpse of Columbus. What are we to do with all these corpses? Let us lock and double-lock the tomb of the Cid. Let us keep him from springing out of his tomb again on horseback, off for new adventures!"

On another occasion, Costa bellowed: "In order to save the sick patient, Spain, the usual drugs will not suffice. 'Surgical politics' are needed and an 'iron surgeon' familiar with the anatomy of the Spanish people, who must also feel love and sympathy for them."

"But what methods do you propose? What is your program?" they asked him angrily.

"School and bread!" the fiery prophet answered tersely. "To educate the people and rectify our economic affairs. We are a backtracking, poverty-stricken, illiterate people. Our economic affairs, both public and private, are in a pitiful condition. We know neither how to earn nor how to spend. The honor and security of a country are not in the hands of the army. They are in the hands of the people who till the soil, work in the vineyards, shepherd the flocks, produce the metal, toil away in the ships, drive the trains and print the books." Often he used to say: "Great are the shortcomings of our race. If we do not correct them quickly, we are doomed. Look to Europe! Take lessons from Europe!"

For modern Spain the vigorous lion of Aragon, Joachim Costa, was a kind of John the Baptist. Like the biblical prophet, this precursor of the Spanish Renaissance cauterized the passions and malice of his contemporaries. He too saw chastisement hanging like a sword over the heads of his brothers. He too cried out in the wilderness: "Repent! Repent!" And, as so often in human history, the wilderness cocked its ear and listened.

The second prophet of the Spanish renaissance, Angelo Ganivet, was the absolute opposite of Joachim Costa. The Lion of Aragon was answered by the voice of the Andalusian nightingale—harmonious, passionate, sweet.

Angelo Ganivet was born in the voluptuous city of Granada. Slender, dark-haired, he had the finesse of an old-fashioned Arabian. Even while very young, he always had a book in his pocket—almost always Virgil or Horace. He used to enjoy calm discussions on philosophical and political themes, in the warm gardens of the Alhambra.

At the age of twenty he came to Madrid and became acquainted with the intellectual aristocracy of the capital city. When he opened his mouth to speak in the Café Levante, near the Puerta del Sol, all his friends listened to him in delight, admiring his wisdom and the sweetness of his voice. Ganivet was refined, worldly, open-minded. He loved life and its joys. He gave untiringly of himself and was destined to commit suicide because of a woman. At the age of thirty, he threw himself into the river in Riga, where he had been sent as consul, and so drowned.

Contrary to Costa, Ganivet studied and extolled the virtues of the Spanish race. He loved passionately the popular ballads as well as *Don Quixote*. He deeply believed that the Spanish people, on the basis of their good qualities alone, would be capable of creating a civilization different from, deeper and more human than the modern civilization of Europe. "We are a house," he wrote, "with two doors: the Pyrenees and Gibraltar. The one door opens on Europe, the other on Africa. A Spanish renaissance can come about only when we concentrate all our forces and energies within our own house. We must close with lock and chains and bars all the doors through which the Spanish spirit has escaped, scattering itself to the four winds." The harsh fanatic Spaniard of Aragon turned his eyes toward Europe, and from her awaited salvation while the delicate, cultivated, utterly Europeanized Ganivet scornfully turned his back on Europe and pledged Spain to remain true to her own character.

Ganivet was a complex spirit, rich and contradictory. He himself admits this with great bitterness: "In the depths of my humble personality there is a shameful dualism—instinct makes me start from underneath, love moves me to look upward, and I remain suspended in between. My position is horrifying. Both those I leave behind me and those I have in front of me are unbearable for me. And those who are in the middle seem to me worst of all." An aristocrat, Ganivet looked on the people as an artist does. He loved everything the people created and experienced: songs, embroideries, dances, festivals, costumes. "A folk song," he used to say, "touches my soul far more deeply than a poem of genius." And somewhere else he wrote: "The roads and villages and cities have a voice and speak. Sometimes I hear them and they say: 'There is no soul here, for there is no work of art to give a purpose to and justify all these stones and plots of earth and tiles.'"

Ganivet was an enemy of the Catholic suffrage movement. He considered the Spanish people uneducated, backward, and he was afraid that political liberties might harm them. "It is utopian to speak of democracy in Spain. Our natural government, like our own idiosyncrasies, is a cruel, strong, authoritative power. We find democratic philanthropy humiliating, since we are all kings in our own houses and in our internal lives. However, I am not appealing for a dictator of genius to save Spain. That would be an artificial head stuck onto the body of the nation. And when he left, he would leave us in a state of still greater collapse."

Ganivet sought the salvation of his country in a deeper, more intrinsic way: "If I were asked to reform a nation, I would unhesitatingly, before anything else, try to reform the relationships between men and women. Then the family and society and nation would soon reform themselves." But Ganivet died young and did not have time to leave a deep influence on his country. He was excessively sensitive and dedicated to his own inner life. He lacked the harsh virtues and psychological coarseness that stamp men of energy. He was a delicate "sculptor of himself." As he said of himself: "Creator of my own immortal soul; sculptor of myself with the chisel of pain; alone; without God—that is what I have been."

Unamuno is the greatest prophetic personality of modern Spain[*]—a stubborn Basque, narrow-minded, passionate, with explosive forcefulness and sanchoesque humor. He has no love for ideologies, abstract meanings, games of the idle polymath mind. His love is for "flesh and bones" man. Behind philosophy, he seeks the philosopher who crystallized it. Behind the pages of a book, he seeks the author and him alone.

---

[*] Unamuno died in 1936.

Papers are for goats. For Unamuno, real and vital people use paper only to leave smudges on.

The famous dilemma—whether Spain should become Europeanized or contained within her own borders—was solved by Unamuno in an unexpected way, but utterly characteristic of him: Europe must be Spanified! "We are Africans," he expostulates. "We are not sarcastic wits and mathematicians, like the Europeans. We are not scientists. We use the things discovered by them: electricity, the railway, the telephone, etc. But our spirit is different: we are mystical and tragic. Our inability to adapt ourselves to European culture will give us the strength to create a new culture of our own. We are not able to play and make a spectacle of life. If a Renan were born in Spain, we would throw stones at him, and I would throw the first stone. I thank you, my God, that you made us neither sarcastic nor skeptics, nor sportsmen nor scientists!"

So Unamuno's message transcends the political or national ideals and becomes religious. Unamuno is trying to give man a new conception of his destiny and a new cosmology that will combine passion, visionary power and realism. The center of Unamuno's struggle is the relationship of the individual with God. "This is the grand, the terrible problem," he says. "If Spain wants to be saved, she must solve this problem. Not in a European way, however, but in a Spanish way. And then Spain and all the world will be saved. Life is not logic or a game; it is religion. There is something far higher, far deeper than logic and the Idea and scientific truth— immortality. However, not in the philosophical sense of immortality—I mean the personal, flesh-and-bones immortality of the individual."

Unamuno's preaching was destined to exert tremendous influence on the Spanish spirit. Precisely because it seems to us so eccentric, idiosyncratic, changeable, has it had such deep influence on a nation, where for centuries this problem of the inner struggle, the relationship of the individual with the divinity, has been the heart, consciously or unconsciously, of the whole spiritual life.

Unamuno is neither the wisest man, nor the most open-minded, nor the greatest writer or philosopher of present-day Spain. But he is something more than all this: he is the most palpitating faithful incarnation of the age-old Don Quixote.

The greatest philosopher in Spain today, and one of the greatest of our age, is the fourth grand prophet of the Spanish renaissance: Ortega y Gasset.*

At the time when the new propaganda for salvation began, Ortega was still very young. He had just returned from Germany, where he had been a pupil of the great German philosopher, Hermann Cohen. Ortega is an enthusiastic worshiper of European wisdom and clarity of mind. He is convinced that only by adapting Spain to the scientific methods of Europe can she be saved. There is no other road to salvation. European logic must purify Spanish passion.

Ortega was born in Madrid. His family was intellectual, the publishers of the newspaper *Impearcial*. Somewhere he remarks that literally: "I was born on top of a printing-press cylinder." And Ortega does indeed have the insatiable appetite of a journalist. But he also has the profundity of a great philosopher. With close attention, he observes everything connected with life: the people around him, economic, political, and social systems. Unamuno scorns the ephemeral life around him and seeks the eternal. Ortega finds the eternal in everyday life. He is struggling to create a new generation of intellectuals, capable of fusing the chaotic richness of

* Ortega y Gasset died in 1955.

the Spanish spirit with the refinement and sharpness of the European intellect. Ortega's preaching is the opposite of Unamuno's: science, logic, systematic work, perfectly up-to-date technique, close contact with Europe—this is his road to salvation.

Which of all these apostolic voices will prevail? None of them alone; all of them together. For each of them has emerged from the vitals of the versatile rich Spanish character and represents one side of the Spanish necessity and reality. All these voices in unison, struggling, feeling sympathy, working together, will direct the Spanish destiny, each one from its own sphere.

The Iberian Peninsula is still seething with a plethora of blood types from the most diverse of races. They have not yet been digested so as to mold one stable type—neither in body, nor in spirit, nor ideologically. This is a great treasure, for there are more abundant possibilities and more unexpected solutions. Yet it is also a great danger, for the discipline to follow a joint end becomes a most difficult feat.

Wandering through the streets of Madrid, I felt joy in discovering a different race lurking behind each form. As I chatted with various representative types, I found to my delight the same heterogeneity in their spirits and ways of thinking. It seems the Homeric tradition is true: that here was the site of the Elysian fields—Paradise—and that all races crossed over the mountains and seas in order to conquer this pagan Land of Promise. Traces of them are still visible in the faces and souls.

The Basques: stubborn, strong, with the arrogant conviction that they are the first mysterious settlers of the Iberian land. The Catalans: practical, industrious, utterly rationalistic. The inhabitants of Galicia, on the borders of Portugal, with their tender lyrical disposition and their gentle day-dreaming spirit. The Castilians: the old *hidalgos* and princes, the brave, poor, proud creators of the great Spanish glory. The Andalusians, with their warm, pleasant climate and their pathos-steeped souls—sensual like the Arabs, uneducated yet cultivated, lazy, yet at the same time, in their passionate moments, fierce, anarchic, fiery. Finally the Mediterranean races along the coasts of Valencia: the Levantines of Spain—gay, covetous, superficial, effeminate spirits that form such an agreeable contrast with the masculine harshness of the Aragonese.

One evening I was going down the main street of Madrid in the direction of the Prado. The full moon had risen among the trees. It was perfectly round and serene, enormous, lighting the thousands of strolling men and women. I shall never forget the unendurable bittersweetness of it. There are moments when love for humanity becomes so overpowering that the individual feels himself melting away, disappearing. The evening breezes smelled of the Prado gardens and the scattered scents of the women. Spring had come. A nightingale sounded suddenly among the flowering chestnut trees. Those superb verses of Góngora rent my heart:

> *This nightingale is wailing*
> *with such rich and wondrous grace,*
> *he seems to have a thousand other*
> *nightingales all warbling in succession*
> *in his breast, and through his throat*
> *their grief.*

All of a sudden, how I loved all Spain that moonwashed evening. I embraced all her sorrows and hopes and longed to see her salvation. Tonight, how clearly and with what horror, I could see the struggle of man over the thin muddy crust of the earth! For a bit of light to shine, the powers of darkness have to clash for centuries. For hope to be born, despair, sorrow, injustice have to be at work for centuries. There is no other way. The good people and the delicate abandon the battle in anger and disgust. If these were the creators of life, they would have cut it along the patterns of philanthropy and their own reason. But life is created by harsh contradictory spirits, steeped in sorrow, patience, obstinacy. And so life radiates the keen smell of tears and sweat and earth.

The nightingale trilled on over all this ephemeral struggling human mass. With the thousands of other nightingales inside it, it could conquer and create harmony. I wished that all the souls of Spain could find a similar harmony, like this nightingale.

■ TOLEDO

■ TOLEDO LIVED in my mind just as El Greco had painted it in the storm: towering, ascetic, scourged by sudden flashes of light, with the arrow of her marvellous Gothic Cathedral, like the arrow of the human soul piercing God's thunder-laden clouds. Half her towers, half her ramparts, half her houses lit with the bluish glint of lightning; the other side collapsing into the abyss in utter darkness. Toledo rose in my mind identical with El Greco's spirit: pierced by light on the one side, pitch dark on the other; unapproachable, on the heights of endeavor, where, as the Byzantine mystic said, lies the starting point of divine madness, not apathy.

But when I reached Toledo and began climbing her narrow little streets, it was a peaceful pleasant morning. The womenfolk were coming back from the famous Arab piazza, Zocodover Square, their baskets full of vegetables and red peppers. The heavy bells of the Cathedral were striking with a deep tired voice. The houses were open, streaming with light, and inside the cool inner courtyards, little girls were watering their decorated flowerpots. As is often the case, the terrifying contact did not come in the form of a thunderbolt or a blaze of fire or a great idea. It came like a gentle spring breeze.

What a pity to seek picturesque ruins and romantic retreats in the famous old cities, along with all the other painted stage effects, where our whorish imaginations like to revel and blare. It is very hard to see a place with our own eyes when a great poet has passed through the place before us. Spain is the discovery of a few poets and painters and flamboyant tourists. Ever since, the mantillas and bullfights and castanets and gypsies of Granada and cigarette girls of Seville and gardens of Valencia have been firing our imaginations.

I am struggling to detach myself from this yoke. As the lives of the saints express it, there are two invisible spirits sitting on man's shoulders. On his right shoulder sits the angel and on his left, the devil. That morning I was aware of the two spirits gazing at Toledo and debating.

The devil on my left, with his thin-pressed sarcastic lips, stammered: "So this is the imperial city, the famous Toledo we so longed to see! Is this plump, overstuffed nursemaid the wondrous Cathedral? Is this dust-covered, flea-bitten bridge the vaunted Alcántara? Where are the cities we have seen that made our hearts dance? Remember Jerusalem, Mycenae, and Moscow! Remember Samarkand and Bukhara! Remember Jaroslav and Novgorod and Assisi! And then make sure you are not fooled by romantic swoonings. Such filthy roads, such ugly women, such insufferable flocks of tourists, such humdrum! Let's get out of here!"

But the angel with his calm sweet voice murmured in my right ear: "Let's go see El Greco!"

I was in no hurry. For I knew very well how pleasant it is to stand near the gate of delight and delay stretching out your hand. I passed El Greco's house in Ovriaki. The big gate was open and I stood at the threshold: a peaceful garden, warm, neglected; a pomegranate tree in bloom, flowering like a blaze of fire; two or three thistly fig-trees; an ancient marble statue. The ivy had taken root and was consuming the walls. A wrinkled old woman sitting in the sun, all stooped over, was cleaning mustard plants. She was just like

an old Cretan woman. In the back of the garden there was
a terrace supported by high columns, and over the terrace,
a window with crisscross iron bars—El Greco's house. The
old woman raised her head, looked at me indifferently and
bent over her mustard plants again. Warm, fragrant serenity,
all Crete rose in my mind, and I could no longer restrain myself. I crossed the entrance and went in, crouched down
near the old woman, picked up a conversation with her.

"Where was El Greco born, Granny?"

"How should I know, childie? They say he came from over
the seas."

"Did you know him?"

" 'Course I did. But I was very young. I don't remember
him."

"And what was El Greco, Granny?"

"He was a man who made Christ and the Apostles!"

I promised to bring her some coffee and sugar if she'd tell
me the truth. The old woman was delighted. Her yellow
cheeks turned rosy and she whispered confidentially:

"He was the man who brought the Americans."

I sprang up in delight. I had never dreamed that the op-
portunistic starving masses could characterize their great
heroes so simply and so graphically. He who brings the Americans is a hero, for with them come baksheesh and pros-
perity. Sure of himself, bent on profit, his feet firmly on the
ground, the peasant sees and judges everything in terms of
his belly.

One day, I remember, I was walking along the banks of
the Akelous River. A peasant in a dirty *fustanella* kilt had
gone ahead as my guide. He had small clever eyes. Suddenly
a bluebird flew over us. Its belly shone dark turquoise, its
wings dark blue. It flashed for a moment with steel-like
reflections, then disappeared among the reeds. I let out a

cry of delight and grabbed my guide's arm: "What's the name of that bird?"

I shall never forget how scornfully that man of Roumeli turned around and stared at me. Then he shrugged his shoulders and muttered: "Why do you go troubling your head over that, you poor boy! You can't eat it!"

The peasant did not give a name to this bird, because it could not be eaten. But to the other bluebird, El Greco, he gave a name. I came out of El Greco's garden. Low and muddy, the Tage River rolled along slowly in the sun. Its banks were bare; its rocks gray and pointed, without a single green leaf. I let my eyes play over them slowly and thought happily that El Greco's ecstatic mad eye must surely have loved these ascetic rocks very much. I was excited, as though I expected to find him still there gazing at them, with sparks in his eyes.

I wandered around El Greco's house and the museum and churches, where his works are. His whole life and struggle were alive in my mind. My eyes were dazzled by the sharp fervent mouths and pale hands with long fingers like starfish, and the fiery-fixed eyes. All these delights lay before me, impatient to enter into me and assume expression. I too was impatient, but restrained myself. For I knew that as soon as the instant of perfect contact comes, then desire (I mean, supreme pleasure) dies.

I moved to and fro in the narrow little streets, and my mind galloped back to the past, in delight. On the eighth of April 1614, on just such a gay morning as this, the door to the great Cretan's house stood open. Little children dressed in white lacy blouses were standing in the doorway with yellow torches in their hands. The proud mysterious foreigner from across the seas, who had come some forty years ago, had died.

All Toledo mourned him. That day the legend created by the vehement taciturn Cretan came to life again on everyone's lips. His life had been strange, his words few and like the blows of an ax. Was it not he who had said of Michelangelo: "A good person, but he didn't know how to paint." Was it not he who had made the wings of his angels so huge that the Church trembled? Was it not he who once wrote on paper: "I cannot stand it any more! How weary I am!" And when the Holy Inquisition questioned him: "Where have you come from? And why did you come?" he answered: "I do not have to give an account of myself to any man!" When he ate, he had musicians in the adjoining room play for his pleasure so that he could enjoy his meal. "He squandered his ducats," said his friend Josef Martínez, "squandered them on splendid things for his house." In the early evening, he loved to visit the gardens of the Cardinal Santoval y Rojas. Olive trees, orange trees, pine trees, fish pools, exotic birds, nude statues of women. There he used to mix with his friends: the poets and monks and warriors and cardinals. These gardens were also frequented by the most cultivated ladies of Toledo, who as Grazian remarked: ". . . say more in a single word than an Athenian philosopher in a whole book."

Toledo had cast its spell on him. It was the city that suited him: still full of grandeur and splendor, but having begun to collapse and fade. However, all the knights and nobles and fierce cardinals and pale monks were still alive—all the passionate ghostlike forms that enchanted the dark strange eye of the staunch Cretan. They all still walked her narrow streets, proud and weary, full of mystic exaltation. His veins throbbed with the finest Arab blood. These same Arabs, who had seized Spain, had also spread as far as Crete—"that island flowing with milk and honey." When they had landed, they burned their ships so they would be forced to conquer it. The same blood of the same Arab conquerors flowed in Cretan and Spanish veins. And when El Greco came to Toledo, he found his real homeland. Unlike the Spanish painters, he still had a virgin eye, for he was seeing the spectacle of Spain for the first time, suddenly, at the critical peak of his youth: all the ecstatic pale faces of Spain; the stern bitter aspiring of a race whose sun had already begun to set.

At the same identical moment, Cervantes was immortalizing these Knights of the Woeful Countenance, with both his tears and his laughter. But El Greco discarded the ephemeral comic elements. Using these same weary aristocratic wayfarers as a point of departure, he succeeded, by his line and color, in crystallizing an eternal phantom: the indestructible despairing soul of man.

Old churches, ruined palaces, a fragrant honeysuckle rearing its tiny head among the ruins: I found myself back in old Ovriaki, at El Greco's house, and I went in. The moment I saw the paintings, I caught my breath. One sweeping voracious glance at them and I had devoured all the brilliant colors and pale spirit-consumed flesh. And as is my habit in my moments of great joy or grief, I forced myself to pretend indifference. In these terrible moments, I need to play; to distract my mind a bit and give it time to comprehend that even the greatest joy or grief is but a phosphorescence shimmering around our bones for a fleeting moment. So it is not worth breaking our hearts over.

I turned to the old museum guard and started talking and joking with him. As I chatted and laughed, my heart felt a bit lighter. Then I grew silent and began looking at El Greco.

All the apostles surrounded me. Suddenly I felt I was falling into the flames. The apostle Bartholomew dressed all in white—his black curly head, pale and hungry, moving like a flame, almost floating off his neck. In his hands, he holds a knife with such airy lightness and grace that he seems to be holding a feather, ready to write. By his side, John, with his curly red hair, both flowering youth and woman in one: a mystic androgyne, holding a chalice that brims over with snakes. The aged Simon, with his sunken cheeks and ineffably sad eyes, with a warrior's spear on which his whole body leans, resting on it so he will not fall. His gaze conveys the irremediable sadness and futility of the struggle.

All the apostles are on fire. At the entrance is the marvelous image of Toledo, and George, El Greco's son, in front holding an unfurled map. And descending from the sky over Toledo, a host of angels, with the Virgin in their midst. They seem to dance, suspended in mid-air—like an erotic swarm of bees in springtime, with the queen bee enthroned amid their fuzzy bellies. An angel falls from on high, headlong like a shooting star.

I recalled El Greco's *Resurrection* in the museum at Madrid. In the ground plane, the guards—yellow, greenish, blue—flop down on their backs. Out of this motley mad human mass rises the Christ all in white, straight as a long-stemmed lily. A godlike arrow soaring through the sky, transcending weight and substance and death. And then, the martyrdom of Saint Maurice gleaming like polished enamel in the midst of the cold Escorial. The three panoplies in front: steel-blue, deep turquoise and yellow; the green dress of the child; the other-worldly rays that beat the air—such exaltation that we seem to have been hurled into a mystic landscape of the full moon.

As with all El Greco's paintings, the light cuts the air like a sword violently. It has something merciless and carnivorous about it, like the Holy Ghost in his *Descent*. There the apostles cower like trembling hares. They want to escape, but it is already too late. The Spirit swoops like a hawk, hooking itself over them. One of the apostles shields his head with crossed hands to escape the Spirit, but his hands are covered with blood.

Such is the light in El Greco's works. It consumes the bodies; dissolves the boundary lines between body and soul; stretches the bodies like archers' bows—even if they break. His light is motion, violent motion. Its source is not the sun. It is opposite to the light of the sun. The light soars as though from some tragic moon. The air shudders with thunder. Sometimes the angels burst in the sky like shooting comets, and break rainbow-colored, threatening, over the heads of human beings. That is why El Greco's faces have the waxy ecstatic look of ghosts or of our own forms lit by some great flash of blue lightning.

El Greco's agony is to find the essence behind phenomena —to torment the body, elongate it, flood it with light insatiably, descend on it and burn it whole. Restless and obstinate, scorning the conventional canons of art, dedicated only to his own vision, he seized his brush in the same way as the knight seizes his sword, and set out. "Painting," he used to say, "is not technique; not recipes and rules. Painting is an exploit. It is inspiration. It is an absolutely personal energy."

Instead of becoming calmer, cooling down as all people do, El Greco grew wilder the older he became. His pulse beat faster and faster. His "madness" became more and more fertile. His last works, *The Fifth Seal, Laocoön, Toledo in the Storm,* are pure flame. These are not bodies. The human soul has become a sword removed from its sheath, the body. And as the Cretan advanced in age, he dared even this: Man, both soul and body, becomes entirely sword. The body grows more and more ethereal, outstretched, transparent, shining, other-worldly—like a soul.

The mystic alchemists of the Middle Ages used to say: "If you do not extract the body from bodies, you have not mastered anything." El Greco, in his last years, achieved this alchemical feat.

Occasionally a vehement love of the earth wells up from El Greco's bodies. His angels have solid, athletic bodies. They are dark-haired with fine black down on their cheeks and upper lips. Their noses are tilted with infinite grace. In the church of Saint Vincente in Toledo, there is an angel thrusting the Virgin up into heaven with his mighty arms. There is such force and vigor in him that we feel ourselves carried away till our own arms and chest ache; and as we watch him, we ourselves seem to be thrusting the whole earth high into the sky.

El Greco's portraits are so intense they send a chill through us. Out of the dark background, the old knight or cardinal seems to emerge like a spectral mass of air. El Greco felt the human body as an obstacle, but at the same time, the only means for the soul to express itself. That is why he never rejected the body as the Arab designers had done, when they replaced it with abstract geometric forms. What crystallized the body for El Greco was not the play of flesh and light. It was the soul, the invisible soul that had to become visible. That is why so long as we are looking at El Greco's portraits, we feel overwhelmed by metaphysical terror. The dark powers of thought: alchemist, magician, enchanter, exorcist come to our mind. All these people he painted keep intact the same body they had while they were alive; the same foibles; the same clothes. They are the same people, who return in a magic mirror, resurrected by a mighty exorcist. So art recaptures its ancient power of magic to resurrect the dead. But there is no longer any sweetness or innocence or bodily warmth in these resurrected bodies. They have passed through Hell and Purgatory and Paradise and are returning to the earth in the form of other-worldly flames. This is how all his angels and human beings emerge, after having passed through the three levels of El Greco's mind.

The spiritual confessor of Saint Teresa, Father Baniez, remarked: "Teresa is big from her feet up to her head. But from her head up, she is incomparably bigger." This is the dimension, the invisible one, that El Greco was struggling to paint throughout his life.

Why, after two and a half centuries, has El Greco re-emerged from the obscurity into which he had sunk? Why has he nowadays become one of our great leaders? Why do we feel such violent excitement in the presence of no other painter? It is because our era is profoundly similar to the restless, stormy agonized consciousness of El Greco. Like him, the greatest modern spirits are struggling to find the essence behind the phenomena, which are no longer capable of satisfying our desires.

Once again art is beginning to be dissatisfied with external phenomena, is beginning to seek, to find the essence; is abstracting as much substance as possible from physical bodies, is searching for a line, a color, a motion capable of expressing the inexpressible, this being the only thing worthy of expression. Rather than what the corporeal eyes sees, art renders what the restless eye of the soul can surmise within this visible world.

All of us keep some part of Dionysos imprisoned in our hearts. The creator is he who concentrates the whole body of

Dionysos inside his heart. That is why a perfect work of art liberates us. What does this mean: "liberates" us? I mean it crushes our own stifling individuality and joins the limbs of the god that twitch crippled inside us, with all his other parts, dispersed among all men all over the world. So at once we breathe and feel ourselves fulfilled. We acknowledge our brothers and transcend death. For, in looking at the work of art, we sense that everything—man and beast, future and past, life and death—are one.

At the great creative moments of humanity, the aim of art is not Beauty. Beauty is only the means. The aim of art is to reveal this oneness. The aim of art is to bring salvation.

"Creation," you might object, "is a game. Its purpose is neither salvation nor Beauty. The creator is a child who sits and plays at the edge of the sea of mystery. Out of the sand he molds people, houses, mountains, animals. He is playing. When you hand him a purpose, he can no longer play. That is to say, he can no longer create."

Yes, creation is a game, so it seems, for it sings and molds without any immediate intervention of logic. It seems to be a state of mystic intoxication. But deep down, infinite hidden powers are at work that strive with a definite firm purpose not even the craftsman can guess. (If he knew it, the game would no longer be so unselfish. It would cease to be a game.) A woman passes. The craftsman sees her and suddenly, in the twinkling of an eye, everything is laid bare to the creator: the line of her throat; her bosom; the apocryphal history of her ancestors; the whole history of the whole human race. And so the marble, the color, the word, the sound, rush out with passion to save this passing woman. The light in a painting strives with darkness, climbs the staircases, nestles in the corners, limps along the ground, leaps and comes to rest on the forehead of the old wise man. And the whole painting all at once lays bare the whole fate of man, the entire soul of the world, flooded with the tragi-comic powers of good and evil. Out of these lines and shadows and sounds the craftsman, even while he plays, is following, serving an unchanging eternal purpose. As even he himself believes, he is liberating the Spirit. From every perfect work of art rises a cry of pain, joy, hope, strife. And above all, the unchanging cry of liberation.

When an African seizes wood, paints, wings, seashells, and often the skull of his ancestor, and fashions a mask to wear at the ritual dances of birth or death or marriage, he is not making a work of art. Suddenly in the forest, he has seen the evil spirit blowing death over the village. In terror, he has run back and shut himself into his hut and quickly snatched the wood and wings and paints to carve a mask: the face of the evil spirit. He knows that only in this way can he exorcise the evil. Imagine the terror of this savage man who "saw" as he tries to reproduce faithfully the terrible vision. On the accuracy of his reproduction depends the salvation of his whole race.

This agony is also felt today by the craftsmen who are striving to crystallize the demonic spirit of our age. In the blind and cowardly silence, only the craftsman can see and speak out. Only he can hear the noise of the unborn. Only he can struggle to divine the Spirit and make it visible. In making it visible, he gives meaning and coherence to the agony of his own age. He liberates the Spirit from ignorance and terror.

The craftsman is the vanguard of God, the ultimate watchtower of His battle line. He is ever struggling to give a new face to the future. The old no longer satisfies his heart, for the creator's heart is never satisfied . . . for his heart and God are one. (And when I say "God," I mean the Power that always gives us more than we are able to receive and always asks for more than we are able to give). He hates everything that is firmly fixed, stagnant, because he hates the abyss. The craftsman is the champion of the Universe, the only one who dares to do battle with Death. He never wins, nor does he ever lose. Sometimes he senses that Death too is an angel of God, who descends from heaven or ascends from the earth (it's all the same) to make his hands strong in battle and to keep him always wide awake.

This agony of the craftsman erupts most violently in fertile transitional periods like our own, and like El Greco's. Naturally such creators are considered madmen by their prudent contemporaries. For twenty-four hours, any man is considered mad if he has seen twenty-four hours before the others. El Greco was considered mad for two and a half centuries. Only now that we are consciously experiencing his agony is El Greco beginning to be acknowledged as one of our leaders. When we have attained the new balance we are striving to find, El Greco will once again become incomprehensible to the tranquil, balanced new generations.

And then later, he will shine again, so following the undulating rhythm of human life over the face of the earth.

■ CORDOVA

■ NAKED, TAWNY, uninhabitable, the mountain ranges beyond Toledo. Attic grace and Arab wilderness. Now and then a medieval castle glistening on the peak of the highest hill, with its half-ruined ramparts and bolted fortress gates flung open and its hungry ivy—the last enemy to scale it. In front of the village, a little church with a slender white bell tower. From far off, it looked like a duck stretching its neck. The little white huts followed in back of it like baby ducks on their way down the mountainside. And as the train rushed past, the whole flock came to life and seemed to be rushing headlong in the opposite direction.

Here and there, white stones glimmered in the red earth like white thistles in bloom. No shade anywhere, everywhere raw vertical light. Then suddenly on a peak, I saw the first windmill. Upright, with its shield in front of its winged frame, standing there in the sunlight, it really did look like a medieval warrior dressed in a gray helmet, clad in armor, ready to attack. How rightly Don Quixote took the windmills for giants, and how Castilian was his logic. Shortly others came into sight, at the bend of the hill, all in a straight line, one in back of the other like an army. At a station stop, there was a sudden sound of a deep little stream cackling from stone to stone, like Sancho's laughter.

Next to me on the train sat a short, dark little soldier, eating and drinking away as he leaned out the window. As he

104

watched the windmills, he began to sing. It was a pathetic song, fraught with love and death, and it had a monotonous heart-rending melody. His voice trembled, high-pitched, provocative, like the voice of a Moslem prayer-caller in the sword-shaped minarets; an old Moorish ballad from the time before the Arabs and Hebrews had scattered from Andalusia. And now it came back to life on the Christian lips of this black-haired soldier:

> *I dreamed a dream last night,*
> *a tiny dream of my soul:*
> *I was holding my love in my arms.*

> *Then suddenly I met a pale pale*
> *lady, more icy cold than snow:*
> *"My love, how came you here? Where*
> *have you come from, dear life?*
> *The doors barred; the windows latticed."*

> *"I am not Love, O my beloved.*
> *I am Death and sent by God."*

> *"Ah, cruel Death, let me*
> *live still one more day."*

> *"I may not leave you one whole day.*
> *One hour only may I grant you!"*

> *Swiftly as the wind he dressed.*
> *Swiftly down the street he flew.*
> *"Open the door, my dove.*
> *O open the door, my lovely lass!"*

"How may I open, for my
lady mother's not asleep!"

"If you do not open now, tonight,
you'll never open for me any more.
Death's after me.
Ah, could I but die by your side!"

"Straightway, I'll open you my window,
and throw you down a silken rope, and
if it doesn't reach you, love, I'll
throw you down my own long hair."

The fine rope broke,
and Death appeared:
"We must go now, love; for
that hour I gave you is over."

To the accompaniment of this plaintive bitter melody, we were coming into the fragrant plains of Andalusia. The landscape began to turn more gentle. There were gardens. The fields glistened. The heat was spreading and the train compartment began to reek of foods, fruits, human sweat. The wide-brimmed sombreros appeared more often. The eyes grew more languorous, the noses were hooked, and the belts were all bright red. In one village planted amid gray clods of earth, a woman emerged from her hut. She was wearing a porphyry-colored shawl over her shoulders, and the whole ash-gray landscape was stamped with this hue, like a royal scarlet seal. This is the delightful miracle in Spain, as in the Orient: just in the instant of feeling suffocated, there is a sudden color, a sudden whiff of jasmine, a song—and the heart leaps for joy and everything else is forgotten.

Peasants kept getting on the train. Full generous lips; shaven sunburned heads. The train compartment filled with cantaloupe and watermelon rinds and banana peels. The chatter broke, then blended. Women in their black mantillas laughed. The old men, not speaking a word, thin as skeletons, like tormented apostles returning from the far ends of the world, leaned their chins on their sticks, and cast their eyes down. No one was reading; not even a newspaper. These Andalusian eyes convey life, finesse, a spontaneous culture. There is no intellectual curiosity or anxiety in them.

The first palm trees came into sight. Slender proud patterns against the deep blue sky. The fruits were more abundant, the gardens more fragrant, the rhododendron bushes more resplendent. The hours grew slower, endless with desire. When would we ever reach Cordova! Leaning out the window in my impatience, I murmured softly the verses of the fiery young poet Lorca:

> *Córdoba.*
> *Far and alone.*
>
> *Black pony, great moon,*
> *and olives in my saddlebag.*
> *Although I know the roads*
> *I'll never get to Córdoba.*
>
> *Over the plain, through the wind,*
> *black pony, red moon;*
> *Death is staring at me*
> *from the towers of Córdoba.*
>
> *O what an endless road!*
> *O my courageous pony!*

Oh, but death awaits me
before I get to Córdoba!

Córdoba.
*Far and alone.**

All the pleasant, gentle Arabic civilization of Spain with
its human warmth rose in my mind. Andalusia had been a
garden full of artificial water canals, where rice, sugar cane
and cotton were grown. The Arabs loved the earth, trees,
flowers. They were the first to bring camellias to Europe, as
well as jasmine, apricot trees and peach trees, orange trees
and dates. They were also renowned craftsmen in iron and
leather. No race ever constructed such pliable, indestructible
swords, such delicate, impenetrable armor. And they were also
master craftsmen in silks, china, sweets, and perfumes.

Set among such gardens, the Spirit was also cultivated
and decked itself out, building its nest and warbling happily
in this "Athens of the West": Cordova. The Library of Cordova had 400,000 volumes and specialized scholars translat-
ing Greek wisdom into Arabic. Who is not familiar with the
great Cadi of Cordova, Averroës? Doctor of law; philosopher;
medical doctor; commentator on Aristotle; and astronomer.
He fought the great battle to reconcile theology with science.
And if only this single phrase of his had survived he would
deserve to be immortal: "Any moral system based on the
hope of reward and the fear of punishment is unworthy of
man and God: It is immoral!" The pride and dignity of the
Arabs; the nobility of their race; the unselfishness of the invincible spirit which does not do good for the sake of being
paid, and does not avoid evil because of being afraid! When

* Translated by Willis Barnstone.

will man be capable of founding his virtue and his faith on this kind of disinterested spirit? Perhaps never, for never will man be able to liberate himself from hope and fear.

Here in the royal Arab courts, the poets were in the ascendancy. They were not parasites and buffoons, as they were among the Byzantines and the Franks. They were the close friends of the king, his consolers and drinking companions, his private soldiers, who conquered the most immortal provinces. The Caliph al-Mu'tasim said to his poet, "When I hear you sing, I seem to see the borders of my kingdom spreading." They loved all the good things of this world—flowers, women, wine. The poet Muslim hails his brimming cup of wine: "It is our young queen. Her father was a magician. And longing for our kiss, she turned Mohammedan. We asked for her in marriage, and lo, here comes the matchmaker. Walking with sober and official gait, he brings her to us."

And as usual with the great Eastern spirits, here too the Arabs fused opposites which Western minds find so hard to absorb: delight in the pleasures of life, ever-present food and drink, indolent caresses—combined with a fierce militaristic temperament: "Throw yourself into the heart of battle," sang one of their poets, "when even the most fearless lads retreat and lose their daring! And whenever a difficult feat arises, place all the responsibility on yourself!"

The Andalusian gardens were like happy Theban retreats for the Arab mystics. Hence they set out on their grand journey to God, passing through the five stations, one by one. The first of all: "The Station of Abnegation," where they deny themselves and no longer want the pleasures of this earth. They reach the "Station of Adoration," where, unselfishly and humbly, they adore Allah, without asking any reward of Him. Thence begins their journey to heaven. No longer immersed in theory, they now live and walk and act. So they reach the fourth, "The Station of Annihilation." Now they sacrifice their outer and their inner lives to Allah, and in this way they reach the peak of their ascent: "Life after Annihilation." Now man has reached Kutb, or union with God. He has become Faana, or the axis of the world: the polar star.

So for seven centuries, the Arabs watered the land, decorated the stones, embellished their souls. But their labors were like spring clouds that scattered. The civil riots came. The Christians came. The canals that watered the earth clogged up. The gardens withered. The fountains ran dry. Art, song, women were now regarded as mortal sins. The new moon had set. Cordova was now in darkness, and her splendor no longer lived except in the memory and imagination. On the stormy shore of time she faded like sea foam. As the poet Farid ud-din Attar put it:

> She donned the cloak of Nothingness,
> Drank from the glass of Annihilation,
> Shrouded her bosom in Unconsciousness,
> And wrapped herself in the linen of Nonexistence.

Of all this shimmering play of light over the Andalusian plains, what survived? A miracle. The Mosque of Cordova: the *Mezquita*—Mohammed's cool and shady house with its eight hundred and fifty columns.

It was already early evening when I reached Cordova. The air had turned a bit cooler, and it was possible to breathe freely again. A fragrant smell wafted from the little house-gardens. Along the wide Bulevar del Gran Capitán, all Cordova was taking its slow evening stroll. How shall I ever forget that hour? My head felt light and a bit giddy. The air had a tepid, dense smell about it, as on entering a closed Oriental garden. I turned around to look: all the women had sprigs of jasmine in their hair.

Their transparent black mantillas floated lightly over their high combs. In the twilight, their eyes shone velvety, flooded in shadow. Their fans moved ever so serenely over their breasts. They seemed to be singing them a lullaby, as though trying to lull to sleep two sleepless twins. The men were wearing the marvellous sombreros, wide-brimmed, high, stiffly starched. Suddenly this whole square seemed to have turned into a theater where a serious pantomime with a Spanish theme was being performed.

A lame girl passed by, holding a tray of freshly cleaned figs. As she was hawking them, she seemed to be offering them free. She was squint-eyed, and, in her curly Negro hair, she had pinned a marvellous yellow rose. At another street corner there was a little girl, about six years old, staring longingly at a basket of jasmine an old woman was vending. I stopped and bought her a little bunch and laid it in her hair. I shall never forget—not her delight—but the greedy gesture: how she snatched it, fastened it in her hair, then disappeared down the dark narrow streets. On a low balcony, a woman emerged—terribly pale with bright red painted lips and enormous eyes. She was holding a black fan. With a sudden rush, she leaned over. Her whole body seemed to bend as she rested her bosom on the iron railing, staring hungrily down at the men passing in the street.

Mohammed said: "Three things give me pleasure: flowers, women, and above all, prayer." Yet when it is a summer twilight and the women's hair is decked with jasmine, then all three—flowers, women, and prayer—become one.

From an arid hill, I was gazing at the low mountain slopes due north. In the blue twilight, I was trying to make out the blessed peak where the illustrious Sultan Abd-er-Rahman had built his magic palace, Medina az-Zahra, to please the woman whom he loved. In this earthly paradise had lived 6,300 women, 3,750 children, 12,000 guards and eunuchs dressed in silk. The ceilings were wrought of cypress wood and gold and mother-of-pearl; the walls of transparent marbles and gold mosaics. There were endless gardens. Each one had some 14,000 identical trees: pomegranate, orange, and apple, and among the trees strolled the warriors and the poets and the women. The poet Amr ibn-Abu-Habbat sang:

> *Here, O Queen, in these gardens*
> *You must sit to welcome Victory.*
> *Welcome the vanquished too,*
> *And let Decision, crowned with happiness,*
> *Stand at your right hand.*

And today, here I was staring at these same mountain ranges; striving to find where the palace must have been. But everything had sunk: gardens, women, wise men and all. Perhaps there is still a bracelet intact somewhere beneath the earth; or some bronze basin with proverbs from the Koran; or some delicate jawbone with small pearl-white teeth. "We are sobs made of flesh, and no one hears us." And yet it is right that we should cry out and rebel; like Don Quixote denying death, even as we die. Tonight it pleased me to imagine Omar Khayyám's infinitely bitter verses on the fine eager lips of Abd-er-Rahman:

Ah, Love! Could you and I with Him conspire
To grasp this sorry Scheme of Things entire,
Would not we shatter it to bits—and then
Remold it nearer to the Heart's Desire! *

Here in Cordova sleep is heavy, dense with haunted dreams. The trap doors of the mind open. Ancient desires turn into ghosts, and in the morning when I woke up, I remembered nothing. Only my mouth was very bitter. My first thought flew to the cool mystic *mezquita* awaiting me. I washed, felt refreshed, took to the narrow little streets with palpitating heart. I asked no one the way, moving with certainty, as though going back to my own ancestral home. Suddenly, high ramparts rose in front of me. A wide half-open door shone brightly in the fiery sun and, behind it, orange trees with cypress trunks and green-black leaves.

How to describe the serene, intensely pleasant excitement that overwhelms you the moment you cross the threshold, walk past the orange trees and sink into the cool half-light, where the columns shimmer like phosphorus? The same delight as the blue beetle must feel at high noon when it crawls head first into a huge rose plant. Above all, the body rejoices. Outside, the unbearable heat: you hadn't been able to breathe. Your eyes had been blinded by the glaring reflection from the whitewashed houses. But then, as soon as you cross the threshold, your eyelids are soothed. Your forehead feels cool, and you feel your whole body sinking into a cool, calm sea. And with the body, the soul rejoices too. You have the sense of entering not the military fortress of the mighty Jehovah or the poor hovel of Jesus Christ. Here you are entering the cool sweet-smelling tent of the dark-

* Stanza 99 of *Rubáiyát* (Edward FitzGerald translation).

haired Prophet, with its straw mats and water jugs and the laughter of a little lady behind the lattices.

There is such an earthy joy here, such balance between man and God. Imagination has come down to earth in the form of everyday reality. God does not come here wrapped in lightning and thunder. Nor do the mountains smoke. Nor does he descend like a poor beggar. Nor is he crucified amid derisive hisses and bloodshed. To this place God comes as a bronze goblet of cold water; as a bird; as the beloved *boulboul*, or nightingale of the East. And that is why we must be always ready. And what is meant by "ready"? A pure heart and a pure, just-washed body. "God," says the Prophet, "does not look with favorable eyes on those who present themselves to him with hair uncombed." And that is why Mohammed always carried with him a comb, a pair of scissors, scented oil for his hair and a little mirror.

In the same way, this marble tent pitched by the Prophet to welcome God is also full of a tender love of life. There is no terror or grief here. You are overpowered by joy. You feel slightly intoxicated as you move in among the low, graceful columns. At every step, your heart feels free to choose, take whichever path it wants. All of them are good, since God is everywhere. You have entered His house. You can no longer lose your way.

It is an absolutely musical sensation that overwhelms you. Straight off, from the first moment, the motif is given you, the simplest of melodies: in between every two columns, an arabesque arch, and over it, another, narrower arch. This motif returns again and again, continually, like an echo. Mathematical precision combined with ecstasy; strict geometrical outline with imagination. Algebra and the Arabian Nights. You rejoice in the spectacle of the human mind governing matter, without losing its lightness and grace.

Through the colored windows stream light and air. The mosque takes on a new color at every shift of the eye: dark cherry, green, blue, orange. The whole mistily-lit temple is a rich, rainbow-colored vision, intersected by the marble columns at equal intervals. These columns are not tall, as in the Gothic churches. Compared with them, a man's stature does not dwindle into insignificance. They are like our sisters, a bit taller than we are, and out of the shadowy darkness, they smile at us. They are made of green, yellow, white marble and precious porphyry. Some of them are Byzantine; others Arabian; others ancient. Up to the level of a man's height, they are polished and shiny, because, for so many centuries, countless followers have been leaning their bodies against them.

I never saw a more joyful or more human temple. It is a triumphant, wholehearted paean to God. Man, like a soldier returning from the war, bears the good tidings to his general: God. And at the very instant of the good tidings, the tent was pitched to welcome God and man.

In the Parthenon, the mind rejoices in the solid logic of man. In the Gothic churches, inside those stone forests that are so very high and dark, you are overcome with fear. You feel that lurking somewhere in the background, behind those columns, the Invisible is crouching like a hungry lion. Here in this mosque, human joy reverberates. Like a conqueror, you move from apse to apse. At every step you take, the shadow and light shift. All our marble sisters sway and seem to dance. Joy; love of the earth; gratitude to Allah for creating all the good things of the earth—fruits, birds, women, war—so marvellously adapted to our bodies and our souls.

I was sitting at the base of a column in front of the sacred Michrab—the Moslem Holy Altar. Here the superb stone and wood carvings are still intact. Among the circumambient carvings glitter proverbs from the Koran, wrought in gilded crystal. Here was the dais of the giant Koran, which Osman had written with his own hand. Decorated with emeralds and rubies, it was so heavy that two men could not budge it. Later it was lost. In the wide area all around it, the stones are eroded, for here the Moslem followers used to crawl seven times over the floor, and so, the stone slabs have all been eaten away.

Transparent marbles, colored crystals, mother-of-pearl, precious woods, silk carpets in winter, cool straw mats in summer, 7,000 tapers and 800 silver candelabra where fragrant oil was burned. Three of these were enormous: each of them burning 40 kilos of oil every night. The bells of Saint Jacob of Compostela had been dragged here by slaves, turned upside down, and suspended with silver chains. Then they were filled and used as candelabra that burned mutely to illuminate another face of God.

I got up from the base of my column. All this Oriental splendor intoxicated my heart. All this joyful contact with God pleased me, like some exotic fairy tale, where you go on opening more and more doors: red ones, green ones, rosy ones, and you go on and on and on, and the magic passageway is without end.

Then suddenly, plunged as I was in fantastic expectation, I raised my eyes: and there in the midst of this beauty, where the human soul had set out to find God (this was obvious), there between two columns, I saw the figure of the crucified Christ—suspended, enormous, covered in blood. Through the shadow, I could see it writhing; the five wounds running; the Virgin fainting at his feet; John opening his mouth frantically, as though he were bellowing.

I could not look at it. The earth is a flower-strewn path

leading us to the grave. It is possible to fill that path, as Christianity did, with little worms out of the tomb, and so no longer be able to delight in any good thing of the earth. Behind the flowers, behind the woman, there will always be white worms creeping there. But it is also possible to keep these inclement messengers at a distance, until their final moment, and so go to the grave without staggering, after having reaped the joys along the wayside. Such is the road Mohammed chose to bring his followers to Allah.

As I gazed at this mosque, which had ended as a church, I moved to and fro, touching the columns. I thought to myself: This miracle will last many centuries more. Will the day ever come when another religion will pass over it, when another face of God (i.e. another face of man) will shine in this shadowy place—with the same joyful heart, only with a freer mind—more liberated from metaphysical hopes? To go to death, knowing that there is no gate whereby to enter Heaven—except the precipice; to know that there is no salvation, and yet not be seized by panic; to feel love of life, pride in being free, joy in having overcome hope and fear . . . When will such a luminous, tender, proud worship of the earth come?

I moved away from the crucified Christ. I felt sad for the mosque: it was like seeing a bright red apple and then suddenly, inside its fresh crisp core, a worm eating it away. I heard hasty footsteps and turned. A girl, with a mantilla and a red fan, was rushing anxiously from column to column. She knelt at every icon, pretending to pray. But her eyes darted slantwise, nervously. She was expecting someone. She moved her fan restlessly, straightened the jasmine on the right side of her hair, moved on to the next column.

All at once, the whole church was full of her agony. The

divine mosque overflowed with human grief. And I too was in agony, suffering with the girl. I too was waiting. And then, there among the columns, the friend appeared, holding his sombrero in his hands, radiating innocence from head to toe. He had a small, hook-shaped mustache. As soon as the girl caught sight of him, she dropped God. What had she to do with Him now? And she ran to her friend.

Happily, I sprang up. Now the mosque had become meaningful. The real everyday God, the human heart, with all its love of the earth, is still the God of the *mezquita*.

■ SEVILLE

Blessed be the joints of my hands, for they are not bony like horses' joints, and so are able to caress you.

And blessed be the thin surface of my lips, for so my blood is nearer yours, when I am kissing you.

And blessed be your long tresses, for when I lift them like a wing, your neck can feel my breath more gentle, and rest more pleasantly upon my arm in our long moments of tranquillity.

Instinctively these erotic phrases of a Spanish poet friend of mine rambled over my lips, as I was entering Seville. I no longer asked myself was it day or night; was there a fine rain falling or was it sunny? I seemed suddenly to have turned into a rose beetle, remembering nothing except perfumed scents and colors from my first contact with Seville. And I rejoiced at my luck in being born into such a brightly colored, fragrant world.

How can man hail the beauty of the earth, except in a piercing cry? When will we open up our eyes and really see a flower; the earth; water; a woman? Really see our bodies that have been created expressly for the world; really see the world that has been created expressly for our bodies, and say with gratitude: "You please me!"

Often when I am wandering alone in foreign cities, I can barely restrain myself from crying out. What is this blessing, this miracle of being alive; of being old; of being thirsty and able to drink water and feeling refreshed through and through; of being hungry and eating a piece of bread and feeling one's bone's crackle with pleasure? And how came it that pleasure is so intertwined, so at home with Necessity?

I was sitting on a rock outside the Arab palace: the famous Alcázar. There was a pleasant sun. Seville was awake now, whirring like a beehive, with her fragrant gardens. It was still early morning, and the palace gates hadn't opened yet. I looked hard at my hands bathed in the early morning sunlight, and they seemed to be holding a golden ball. I touched my head, and it seemed to me like the ark, where all the birds and beasts and gods took refuge to save themselves, sailing over the abyss. That early morning, I blessed and wordlessly sang the praises of my five senses, for now— lo and behold!—the doors of the Arabian fairy tale were about to open, and they would be able to enter.

A noisy white cloud of doves flew up, scattering over my head. And suddenly, by a mysterious process of association, the tender words of the thrice-holy ascetic, Spinoza, sprang into my mind: "No god and no human being, unless he be evil, takes pleasure in hardships and torments. Nor does he consider as virtues tears, sighs, and terror. Quite the contrary: the more we rejoice, the higher we rise toward perfection [viz., the more we participate in the divine nature]. Hear me: It befits the wise man to rejoice and take power from delicious food and drink. It befits him to rejoice in the beauty of the earth, in ornaments that embellish, in music, and games . . . The free man never reflects on death. For him wisdom means to study not death, but life."

A pleasant breeze from Mohammed's paradise that is so like the earth blew over my forehead, and cleared away all laments and dirges. My heart felt liberated from all those gods who groan and frighten and refuse to leave poor man free from fear, to delight a bit in the color, sound, smell, taste of the world during the tiny flash of lightning while he is alive. For a moment, here at the threshold of the Alcázar, I sensed the real wisdom. When I had first read these words of Spinoza in the distant grim city of the North, my heart had not been stirred by them as when I recollected them today. They had seemed to me just black ink on white paper. But today in this hot gypsyish Seville, how suddenly they had come to life, flying off the paper and up over me like doves!

By now, the sun had risen high in the sky. The castle watchman had arrived with his big keys, like a jolly Saint Peter, wearing a broad greenish sombrero and a sprig of jasmine in his ear: *"Buenos días!"*

This is just how I imagine the gatekeeper to the real Paradise: jolly, good-natured, with a sprig of jasmine in his ear. He too would stretch out his hand for you to give him a little tip, before opening the door for you. There would also be days (once or twice a week) when the poor people— the malefactors, the liars, the dishonorable and the miserly —could enter free of charge. "Restitution of all things!" as the tender and merciful (far more merciful than his own God) poet, Gregory of Nazianzus, had once said.

I wandered around the palace on tiptoe, feeling that I was walking on top of thin marble tombstones. And a chill went through me, as though I were expecting at any moment to see the deadmen fly out of the earth, complaining that we tread upon them: "Was not I too once young? Was not I too a brave young lad?"

Slender white columns; finely carved lacy marbles; gilded proverbs from the Koran; marble designs dangling like stalactites; cool fountains . . . One day the Caliph Mu'-tamini's love, the Sultana, had felt like imitating the life of the peasant women. For one day, through her gold lattices, she'd seen them down on the road, trampling barefoot in the mud. So the Caliph Mu'tamini ordered his courtyard to be strewn with ground cinnamon, cloves, and nutmeg, then watered down with orange blossom scent to make mud. And so his love was also able to trample in the mud with her tiny bare feet. . . .

Voices began to lift the tombstone of my memory. But I chased them away so as to be able to rejoice with clear eyes in the living marbles and sage designs surrounding me. I touched them with my hands to see them better, reliving all the mystical Arabian imagination, their patience and their love. I felt the dark-skinned craftsman bent here in ecstasy, all his life long, to decorate this complex limpid dream of his with geometrical precision.

In this place, I sensed with deep joy the fusion of two great qualities: ecstasy and precision. They are so rarely fused, and when they are, they constitute the highest synthesis. A mystical aim, with definite mathematically calculated means. For all this decoration is the dream of a master mathematician. As the line progresses and unwinds, it becomes the abstract expression—the distillation—of all plants, all animals and all thoughts. It becomes the solid geometrical essence of life, emancipated from the ephemeral flesh and its various fluid masks. In this way, the Arabs—at once the great algebra scholars and mystics—succeeded in discovering and crystallizing the essence behind the phenomena.

I abandoned myself happily to this delightful aspect of metaphysics. The same musical sensation was generated in me that I had felt in the mosque at Cordova. All this decoration is a song: monotonous, erotic, always with the same refrain, like a lullaby. And this song is so pleasant, so tender, so familiar to our human hearts from time immemorial, that we feel it is the very voice of the Earth, fraught with sweet and terrifying forebodings.

Then I crossed the "Courtyard of the Maidens." Here the kings of Seville, both Arabs and Christians (all equally moved by the voices of Seville), used to receive as tribute one hundred of the most beautiful girls of their kingdom. "The tyrant served by a whole army of eyes—now tell me, where can he have gone with all that army of his?" Vicious useless questions. Yes, he did go down into the bowels of the earth. Yet, before going down, he had had time to kiss these women and make these eyes weep. Life is not extant. . . . It is a matter of intensity. It is like a thick drop of honey, and the tyrant went away well filled.

I went down into the huge hot gardens: basil, mint, marjoram—all the humble jolly herbs of the family household. I quickened my steps, over through the laurel bushes, near the cypress trees. I was trying to find the site of the baths of the beautiful María Padilla, famous mistress of Peter the Cruel. This must have been where she used to delight in lying stark naked, sparkling in the sun as she felt the men's stares caressing her like hands from the upper windows. And now the beautiful hetaera lies in a church in Madrid, by the side of a king: Saint Ferdinand.

I went back to the palace to take my leave of the slender

ethereal arches and the carvings that twist like rings of smoke. How the beleaguered human soul finds its exodus and leaps over every impediment to speak a word of freedom! The Moslem religion forbade its followers to represent living creatures in painting or in carving. "Woe betide any man who paints a living creature. On the day of the Second Coming, the faces he has painted will come out of the tomb and rush upon him, demanding that he give them a soul. And then, the artisan, unable to give soul to his creatures, will burn in everlasting fire." But in spite of this, the Arabs overcame the harsh ban and found another way for disburdening themselves of the creatures that cried out inside them, longing to assume a shape. By abstract symbolic representation, they liberated their souls.

I went away, rubbing a laurel leaf between my fingers. The fountain had run dry. The followers no longer fixed their ecstatic eyes on the designs, and the designs had lost their divine meaning. This scent of the laurel leaf on my fingertips was the only definite, certain, good thing that survived from all these fair ladies and merciless kings, who had passed like violet shadows over these sun-washed marbles and slender columns.

With this scent still on my fingertips, I entered the renowned giant of a cathedral. It was noontime when I crossed its terrible threshold. My eyes were still dazzled by the jubilant marbles of the Alcázar. Here they felt awestruck. Here they entered the house of another God. Like an ant, I circled around the base of each column. A painting by El Greco, *Saint Francis*, passionate and pale, was shining luminous in the blue shadow. The "pauper of God" holds a skull in his hand. He stares at it, as the mask he will wear to make God laugh, when God finally deigns to send his great marshal, Death, to summon him to His court. In the meantime, throughout this ephemeral life of preparation, Brother Francis holds the skull, his future mask, and studies his role.

Further down, on a wall, Saint Christopher is painted in the act of crossing the river, with the Christ Child on his shoulders. In front of the painting there is a large marble coffin supported by four queens: the tomb of Christopher Columbus. And down on the stone slates are the engravings of the three fateful caravels in which he had launched out to find the New World: the *Santa María,* the *Pinta* and the *Niña.* Only one thing is missing—the most important—to complete the history of the great man: the chains that bound him when he was carried back to his native land from the world he had discovered.

The bitter, tragic fate of Columbus envenomed my mind. He was "drunk with the stars," astride the prow of his ship. Far off to the west, he stared out at the empty sea. He was dissolving—dissolving like the silkworm when it is full of silk and starts spinning out of its own vitals to weave its cocoon. In the same way, this Don Quixote of the sea was spinning the new continent out of his own vitals—creating it, flesh of his flesh, night and day, silently, tenaciously. Till one day the dream was incarnated, and the first birds came into sight, with a few blades of green grass in their claws.

I went down to the banks of the Guadalquivir, the harbor of Seville. Big ships with figureheads and colored keels had cast anchor. And in the wine shop, there was a parrot calling out like a human being. Opposite on the other bank rose the palm trees, elegant and lightly swaying. The marvellous port, where the sailing galleys used to unload the exotic riches of America, was senile now. A few antiquated ships; two or three parrots; a row of palm trees. Nothing else.

Today, Sunday, the women were taking their strolls in the gardens and along the quays. Warm, dark-haired, with the fatal swayings of their hips, they lived up to their legend faithfully. The way they ambled along the quay—plump, painted, with their huge eyes—they looked like the figure-heads on the ships, and seemed to have stepped down from their prows tonight to walk on the earth and stretch their limbs. Surely these must be the Sirens. The age-old idols with the huge buttocks carved in primitive times: with a whirlwind painted between the breasts, or (like an idol from Knossos) with a piece of magnetic iron wedged between their thighs.

The star of Aphrodite had risen up above the sails. People felt released from their daily toil, and out of their vitals soared an erotic song, so bitter that only someone who despised humanity could be unmoved by it. The porters in the harbor; the sailors and the vagabonds and shipmasters; the magnificent beggars; and the rascally bony gypsies, half-naked and greedy, emerged from their little boats, gathering in the narrow sea-washed lanes and moving on toward the quay. A fierce vision burst inside me, kaleidoscopic and primitive, arousing in my blood instincts of the age-old vagabond. Then, when all the street lamps were lit and the hurdy-gurdies had begun to boom, the hungry slave girls of Sea-Born Aphrodite arrived on the scene, painted, perfumed, wanton. They moved to and fro, chattering like wag-tails on the quay. When they grew tired, they sat on the iron posts, where the cables of the little boats were tied. Then they got up again and strutted proudly past the wine shops.

I took two handfuls of white and red grapes and some bananas, and ate them peacefully, happily, standing alongside the sailors and the hoarse-voiced women. I felt like a blissful ascetic, blessing God for sending him grapes and bananas and hunger—and other vagabonds for company.

■ ■

The sun set. The waters turned red as wine, and the ships were laden with blue and rose shadows.

On the quay, there were five or six young girls sitting astride the piles of sacks. They wore shawls of all colors, and roses in their hair. They had been laughing and rambling along, when suddenly their knees seemed to give way and they sat down. A young man, dressed in a violet waistcoat and short black velvet trousers and red stockings up to his knees, was passing back and forth in front of them, whistling derisively.

I recalled the other national hero of Spain: the fearless seeker of women, Don Juan, who was born here in Seville. Here he had carried off the greatest exploits of his love campaigns. And here he was now brought back to life, strolling along the quay on a Sunday.

Don Juan is not the egotistical, sentimental, woman-crazy hero of Europe, who chases woman after woman in his attempt to find the ideal type. Don Juan does not demand perfection and everlasting happiness—only an intense momentary delight. Love may mean blindness and prodigality; may mean fantastic wastefulness. But Don Juan is not in love. He is intrepid and sensual. He does not love in the deep, anxious sense which Northern peoples attach to Love. He is never mastered by his feeling. *He possesses; he is not possessed*—and this is his power. To this union of pride and sensuality he owes all his nobility and warmth. If he were not proud, he would soon have turned into one of Circe's "swine." If he were not sensual, he would have ended up a cold diabolical pander of women, bereft of joy or tenderness. Don Juan does not cry out, like his northern namesake—"I am drowning! I cannot go on!"—at the instant of embracing the woman. He keeps his discipline and balance, goes on for a moment intact—only a moment—and then withdraws again still intact and unwounded. "They will defeat me, unless I defeat them!" he reflects, wide awake at the very hour he is confessing his passion on bended knee. For him, women are a game, but a dangerous game. For Don Juan is profoundly aware of the pleasure they give him. There is only one salvation: flight. But flight, after having won.

Doesn't even God himself use this same system to save Himself from the pleasures of the flesh? He too leaps from body to body; stops a moment to delight; then off again astride his Pegasus, Love. He too saves Himself by fleeing, rushing on into another body. Unfaithfulness, conquest and flight are the three great stages of His journey through the flesh. He is the great Don Juan of Matter, unattainable and sensual, passionate, yet free. The Woman—Matter—clutches him with her two hands and her two feet so that he will not escape. But Don Juan, the Spirit, the wakeful wandering flame, leaps up and does escape.

Don Quixote and Don Juan, these two grand Spaniards, are two of the deepest, most clear-cut masks of God. That is why I felt so happy that evening in the harbor of Seville, when I saw the young man in his violet waistcoat and high red stockings up to his knees. By now he had sat down facing the girls. He began singing a lively love serenade. . . .

The women got up. It was evening now. With the star of Aphrodite tangled in their hair, they walked past the young man staring at them so mockingly. The youngest one, the one with the yellow shawl and black tassels, stopped short. Then secretively, so her friends wouldn't see her, she took the rose out of her hair, and blushing scarlet, threw it to him.

■ GRANADA

■ OVER THE GREAT gate of the Alhambra, the
Moslems hung an outstretched hand to remind their followers of the five paths leading to God: Faith, Mercy,
Prayer, Fasting and the Pilgrimage to Mecca. Of these five
paths, I took the last. Except that I do not know where
Mecca is, and I am seeking it all over the earth. Till one day,
the limpid simple words of an Arab poet will flash inside me
like lightning: "The Mecca you are searching for lies inside
your own heart." Till that day, I shall wander from place to
place, and each time I will think I have at last reached
Mecca. And each time my heart will leap. Then finally, one
day, I shall either reach the end of my journey and rest
motionless at the center of my own heart, serene and happy;
or else—would this might be the case!—not even my heart
will be able to console me, and so the only Mecca left me,
the only sure one, will be the grave. But till that time, let
us walk. Let us be anxious and inconsolable. Let us be
deceived unceasingly. Let us build Meccas and tear them
down! If my heart were opened, one thing only would appear: a stony path with a human being climbing uphill,
bereft of hope.

I am glad that as I entered Granada—walking through
her noisy streets and climbing up to her high gardens; seeing
the plain beyond and the Sierra Nevada with its snowy
peaks, and standing outside the entranceway to the Alhambra

—once again my heart leaped as though it had finally found Mecca. I did not say anything to my heart, so as not to quench its flame. I left it free to believe for a moment, unpolluted by the miserable quibblings of the intellect. I wanted to have time to enjoy the full emotional force. For at the heights of emotion, we have time before we let the mind, that blustery north wind, blow away and shatter the superb mirage in the desert.

I felt a shiver pass through me when I entered the Alhambra and fastened my eyes hungrily on that miracle spread out before me. All these slender columns, ethereal arches, designs, colors, courtyards, water, seemed to me a trick of the imagination. I would blow and they would fade away. As I moved from hall to hall, I felt as though I were entering some incredible Oriental fairy tale; listening to Scheherazade, the human soul, narrate the Thousand and One Nights. And so long as she went on telling the stories, Death held back and did not swoop on her to deaden her tongue. For he too wanted to hear the sequel. I listened and listened as I passed from column to column. And all the bloody legends took on a symbolic bloodless meaning through the transparent mantle of Art.

I climbed up to the tower. There below, the extraordinary vision of Granada unfurled before me: the rich plain and the spectral mountain beyond. My guide was a man of the people. He'd had his fill of all this beauty, and he turned around and nodded to me:

"Up here in the tower's where the kings used to sit. They drank their cool wine and looked on. Down there in the plain the common people used to toil away."

"And was that fair?" I asked, to rouse him a bit.

He thought for a moment, and then came out with this amazing answer:

"For those times, it was fair!"

He could have had but a dim notion of the great laws that change their character and meaning at every turn of history—so that what was once moral and lawful becomes in time immoral and unlawful. We went down to the baths.

"This is where the king used to take his bath, and over there, the queen. In this niche she put her slippers. And up there, on that circular marble balcony, the blind musicians used to sit cross-legged to play for her. If they were not blind, their eyes were removed, for they were not supposed to see."

The Arabic letters, so like designs—snakes, half-moons, flowers—wove in and out along the walls, roguishly, color-fully. In the bath, unwinding slowly like a mesmerized snake: "O Caliph, the blessing of God be with you, and may he always give you Victory!" And over the water tap, decked like a gay garland, the following words: "Yon fountain is the beneficent cloud which rains upon the people. Like unto it are the Caliph's hands when they wake each morn, ap-portioning good things unto his lions: the soldiers!" And everywhere, insistent and piercing, amid the stone decorations and complex geometric flowers, the cry of the Koran: "There is one God, and Mohammed is His prophet!"

I wandered for hours, enchanted, through the legendary castle. I couldn't tear myself away. In the course of my wanderings, I was trying to distinguish clearly inside myself the sources of my joy. For a long time, I sat like the Moslem followers in front of the intertwining arabesques. And there I discovered the sources of the three supreme feelings aroused in me by the Alhambra.

— 1 —

The identity of Architecture and Music. I had already suspected this in the Cordova mosque and in the Alcázar of

Seville. But here it was revealed to me in its clearest, most enchanting form.

The ultimate supreme endeavor of Arabic architecture is to transcend every solid mass. The walls, insofar as possible, disappear; turn into slender columns and arches; or are carved and designed like Oriental carpets. They are freed of weight. The columns become more and more slender, as well as lower. The arches wave ethereally. The decorations become geometric and abstract, like ideas. A single theme is given and this theme reverberates ad infinitum with mathematical precision and fantastic richness. The Arab musician-architects filled space with light and air and color. They had a single extraordinarily daring aim: to transcend matter. To abstract from it all its immobile heavy content, and leave it only its intellectual outline.

Here in the Alhambra, it becomes completely clear how Music and Architecture are united and spring from the same source: Mathematics. An Oriental refrain—monotonous, enchanting, always with the same rich rhymes; a slow sweet Turkish chant, all passion; like this, slowly, mystically, your thoughts begin to undulate if you gaze for long on the Alhambra. Your soul becomes a nightingale, caught and trilling in among these stone branches that seem to blossom as in April. "Only One can conquer—and that One is Allah!" This phrase weaves round and round, gliding like a snake among the patterns, always the same in form and kind. Then it disappears, golden and mysterious, into the shadow. You are overcome by a light giddiness that is crystal-clear and full of eyes. Here lies the beginning of ecstasy, and the essence of Music.

— 2 —

The second supreme emotion begot by the Alhambra stems from the profound connection between Geometry and Metaphysics.

Never had I felt so deeply close to my two beloved mystics, Spinoza and Ignatius Loyola, as here in the Alhambra. Here for the first time, I saw tangibly how a metaphysical idea can be crystallized, not through romantic allegories and idealistic haziness: but through Mathematics and Geometry.

Let us take a theorem of Spinoza: "When the soul examines itself and the force of the energy it possesses, it rejoices. And the more it rejoices, the more clearly it can distinguish itself and the force of the energy it possesses."

Only if you think about this theorem, with all the geometrical clarity of the Alhambra spread out in front of you, can you understand this profound joy of the soul examining itself. And in the process of examining itself, the soul follows the chain of its own desire with chiseled clarity; and following that, so multiplies its joy that it attains ecstasy: the threshold of omnipotence.

In this same way, Loyola led his disciples to ecstasy via the strictest mathematical calculation. In order to see Christ being crucified inside your own mind, in order to become identified and crucified with Him, you need extraordinary clarity, down to the tiniest detail. You must follow Him to Golgotha, and really see the trees and stones along the roadside, and the people with their facial characteristics—young men, old men, their eyes and hands and clothes. You must persist, intensifying your intellect, sharpening all your senses, until you finally create the vision limpidly, with an unbreakable line, as in Geometry. Only thus will you be able to reach the ultimate metaphysical goal of the Christian: to be crucified yourself with God.

— 3 —

The third emotion aroused by the Alhambra is connected with erotic suggestibility. This, to be sure, is the first and only thing that touches even the most superficial pilgrim to the Alhambra. For most people, this emotion crawls along at a low level of sex and melodrama, and is nourished on romantic ravings or makeshift historical sophistries. However, in its deeper sense, this erotic suggestibility rises from level to level, serenely, as in the Platonic theory of love, shifting from bodies to souls, and from souls to the awe-inspiring male and female forces that have created the visible and invisible world.

After you have been observing all these architectural and musical games insistently, the mystery suddenly is laid bare to you: all these marvels consist of just two lines pursuing one another. They move away glidingly. The female line plays and hides itself. The other, the male line, runs behind. Then they come to rest near one another, intertwine, fuse, complete each other in a circle, rest a moment, enshrine themselves in polygons, rejoice as they fulfill each other. Then suddenly, the one line escapes, and the eternal chase begins all over again: agonized, sensual, like a whirlwind.

The Alhambra is the stone embodiment of the *Song of Songs*:

> By night on my bed I sought him whom my soul
> loveth: I sought him, but I found him not. . . . I
> charge you, O daughters of Jerusalem, if ye find my
> beloved, that ye tell him, that I am sick of love. . . .
> Behold, he cometh leaping upon the mountains,

skipping upon the hills. . . . He standeth behind
our wall, he looketh forth at the windows, shewing
himself through the lattice.

With just such erotic agony, the two primeval solitary lines
—the male and the female—pursue each other here, from
the foundations of the Alhambra up to its domes, which
are as round as a woman's breasts. Gradually all the erotic
skeins lose their physical substantiality. Slowly the vision
inside you is freed of human passions. And you are left
with the two clear unbreakable lines that molded the
world: the one impetus of the universe in pursuit of the
other.

And all the while, individual bitterness and pleasure are
becoming more and more generalized. You begin to see
more clearly through the erotic adventures; these two lines,
that are at war here in the Alhambra, form the holy proverbs.
Suddenly everything becomes clear, and you sense that all
this apparent erotic pursuit really has one, and only one,
aim: to assimilate the terrifying cry that pierces all the walls
of the Alhambra: "There is one God, and Mohammed is
His prophet!"

So having passed from Music to Metaphysics and thence
to Love, you rise involuntarily from stair to stair, till you
scale the summits of this apocryphal vision: the whole
battle of visible and invisible forces erupting in the universe
stems from just two opposing forces, which both hate and
love each other and out of which the world was created.

When I passed through the doorway of the Alhambra and
stepped back into the sunlight, I trembled. I seemed suddenly to have emerged from one marvellous world into
another marvellous world. No doorway on earth sunders so

abruptly two such different worlds. Which is the real world? Where is the fairy tale and where is real life? And how is it possible to combine the cruel struggle of everyday life with unyielding Theory born inside the head—invisible, beyond Necessity?

Above the huge fortress-gate of the Alhambra, in a niche on the lintel, stands a multi-colored plaster statue of the Virgin as a young girl, ignorant, holding a baby in her arms. The upper part of her head had cracked, and in the hollow of her skull, the swallows had built their nest. I leaped for joy. One of the apocryphal gospels says: "The trees and birds and waters beckon to us. Lift the stone, and you will see me. Cut the wood and I am within!"

From a distance outside the city, the Alhambra appears for what it really is: a mighty fortress. A harsh castle, constructed for military purposes with walls two meters thick, embrasures once filled with iron-clad warriors, underground passages once stuffed with carriage equipment, and stables once full of horses. And inside: on a delicate surface of the bulky castle, all the delightful games of man—both erotic and intellectual—are unveiled, without in the least emasculating the walls.

Would that our own spirits might be like the fortress of the Alhambra!

■ BULLFIGHTING

■ ANIMALS ARE CLOSER than human beings to the primeval eternal forces of cosmic creation and destruction. They are closer to God. They are His true angels and archangels.

The earliest human beings were profoundly aware of this dark mystery in animals. When a bear or a deer suddenly emerged in front of its cave and stared mutely at them with its ecstatic eyes, the earliest people must have felt a shudder of terror and respect. Religious awe. It must be God, they thought, who, having learned that we are hungry, has come to give us of His flesh, that we may eat and not be lost. And so began the sacred hunt, the conjurors' exhortations, the violent forays with stones and bows. The killing was a magic act; a religious rite; the final adventure of God's flesh.

Thousands of years have passed, and still, as much as ever, man shudders secretly when he comes face to face with the beast. Even to the present day, among primitive peoples and great creators, theology still continues to be deeply rooted in zoology. The bull, the lion, the eagle, and the exotic fabulous bird are still the four evangelists, who bore the great tidings to the earth. And the most evangelical of all, the one who holds the Word most firmly on his shiny back, is the Bull.

Ancient manly races used to make the Bull the center of their cult worship. Between its horns, they wedged the sun. And on its mighty testicles they hung all their hopes. At the

137

great festivals, they grappled with it. The chief priest was the bullfighter, and the knife his ceremonial instrument—the strongest exorcism, for not even God could oppose it. And when the bull bellowed and dropped, the devotees rushed out and began devouring the raw flesh. Such was this primitive Holy Communion, with real flesh and real blood.

The moment I set foot on Spanish soil, I felt the breath of the sacred bull in the air. Occasionally I used to watch it stalking through the noisy streets, in among the painted ladies and the shouting men. It was silent, shiny, a genuine god, its dark eyes spattered with blood. I used to gaze at the crowds moving toward its temple. They were gay, impatient, excited, on their way to a rite as old as time. . . . And then, in the newspapers, I would read the outcome of the sacred rite, this bloody pantomime between God and man.

At first I found it a bit painful to inhale this tangy air of the ritual. I used to stand outside the sanctuaries, not daring to cross the threshold. I felt I wasn't yet up to it, for I did not want to confront the bullfight as a mere spectacle. I longed to be able to arouse inside myself an age-old emotion, so that thousands of years hereafter, my blood could recall how it was once stirred and blessed through this violent contact with God.

Little by little, I was getting closer to my goal. Spain breathed courage into my heart. I saw the crucified Christs with their thick clots of blood, and my eyes grew accustomed to them. I watched the women dancing, and my temples beat like castanets. I heard their breathy voices and the bells and the trumpets. I ate the red peppers and heavily spiced meats. I drank the earthy red wine of Castile. My five senses were growing stronger. I was alone and free. There was no nostalgia fretting away my spirit; no physical passion exhausting my blood. I was neither happy nor remotely unhappy. I was beyond these conventional terms, living moments that contained all happinesses and all unhappinesses, that transcended them and attained a mystical powerful synthesis.

It was then I felt I was drawing closer to God. Then one day at a Spanish port on the Mediterranean, the eve of my departure from Spain, I saw that I was ready to cross the threshold. I had not fasted or drained my blood, as servile religions demand of man in order to make himself worthy of worshiping God. On the contrary, I had made my flesh stronger, till, now, I was capable of battling with it.

I mixed with the other devotees. We were crossing through a public square, men and women advancing together. All the roads were jammed, flooded with our ritual. It was afternoon. The sun was broiling hot, melting our flesh. There was a smell of armpits. The women's hair reeked of jasmine and roses rotting. A heavy stench of humanity: animal smells of sweat and urine. But this seemed to be the right air for the rite—the earliest primeval air of the cradle—and as the people breathed it in, they felt secretly moved.

Soon the temple emerged on the outskirts of the city: a tremendous stone enclosure, like an arena. The gates were wide open. Today the Great God Bull would be at home to visitors. Red flags waved in the breeze. Guards on horseback rode to and fro. A thick dust rose like incense, except that at the doors, instead of candles and frankincense, the vendors were selling fans, pistachio nuts, cold drinks, fruits. Informally, chewing melon-seeds or whistling, the people entered this house of God here. And they were aware of entering His house.

A vast arena freshly strewn with sand. Along the sides, three wooden platforms—the steps where the devotees would sit. Opposite me, the door—the "Beautiful Gate," through which the bull would come. Shouts and laughs and the smell of bodies mixed with the smell of powders and orange peels. Half the theater, where the poor people sat, in the glaring sunlight. The other half plunged in cool early-evening shadow. Brightly colored fans fluttering quickly, as though beckoning to God to approach. All eyes shining expectantly, fastened on the mystic Gate.

Suddenly the trumpets blared, and two horsemen in medieval attire, wearing feathers on their heads, circled around the arena to clear it. The gates opened behind them and the bullfighters began to parade. First the *matador*—the protagonist, the killer, who springs forward at the critical moment to kill the bull. Then the *banderilleros*, who jab long darts with colored streamers into the nape of the neck, the shoulder blades, and the rumps of the raging beast. Then the *picadores*, or horseback lancers, who further infuriate the bull by throwing lances at it. They were all dressed in formal priestly vestments: short pelisses embroidered in silver and gold; silk waistbands; short trousers in various colors. Last of all came the *capeadores*, with their red capes to arouse and mislead the bull. All these priests were young and elegant, and their temple flooded with joy, gay colors, intensely swift music. The parade—both marriage and funeral procession in one— was brought to a close by three mules harnessed with rich trappings, feathers and bells. Anon these mules would drag away the slaughtered bulls, and the horses with their bellies gorged, or, possibly, even human corpses. For sometimes the god refuses to be sacrificed.

Suddenly they all left and only two *picadores* on horseback remained, motionless, hidden in the shady part of the arena. We all held our breath. A moment of deep silence. Then, suddenly, the gateway creaked and out stepped the pitch black, shiny bull . . . calm, good-natured, advancing hesitantly into the middle of the arena. It stopped short. For a moment, as it sniffed the crowd, it felt afraid. Dazed as it was by the sun, it could only dimly see a colored mist in the arena and thousands of burning eyes. It bellowed in exasperation and turned to go back to its pen.

But then, out of the shadow, emerged the first of the two *picadores*, whose white horse began tracing a broad circle around the bull. Then the bull understood. It could no longer go back to its pen. The people had brought it here in order to kill it. Its whole body bent like a bow as it charged on the horse. For a moment its horns flashed straight under the horse's belly. With all his might, the horseman managed to stick his lance into the nape of the bull's neck and get away in time. The bull bellowed from the pain, then rushed toward the horseman. But now the *capeadores* surrounded it, with their red capes waving. The bull veered and rushed on them. But with a light movement, the supple young men stepped out of the way, and the bull butted its horns at the empty cloth in vain.

The bull hesitated, groaned, looked to the right, looked to the left, lifted its aching head, bowed down by the weight of the thousands of human beings jeering at it. It wanted to lie down. It was tired and in pain.

Then the *banderilleros* emerged. One of them stood boldly in front of the bull, staring it straight in the face. He lifted both hands high and jabbed two big darts into the nape of the bull's neck, one with red and the other with green streamers. He bent and stepped aside lightly, in the split second when the bull was preparing to charge him. Again it butted its horns at the air. Before the maddened beast had time to regain its momentum, another *banderillero* jabbed into it two more darts with yellow streamers. Blood was now pouring over its whole back, and the ill-starred bull was leaping up and down, bellowing, all decked in streamers.

It was worn out and stopped short again, with its head bowed. And then out stepped the *matador*, the killer . . . on foot, dressed in gold and velvets and rose silk stockings up to his knees. He was holding a red cape, behind which was concealed a long shiny sword. He stood facing the bull. The bull was now aware that the grand and critical moment had come. It swayed its head slowly, gathering its strength in preparation. The *matador* quivered all over like a lance, following the rhythmical motion of the bull. He too was preparing. Then suddenly, in the lightning-swift second when the bull was gathering itself to charge, the red cape swooped down, and the sword flashed between the man and the bull. All at once, the beast knelt down trembling. It regained its courage, made as though to get up, but its legs folded under it, and it collapsed on the ground. The sword had gone through its heart. It rolled over on its back, shook its legs two or three times in the air, then, biting its tongue, lifted its head, throat upward. Then came the most hateful of the conspirators, for now there was no longer any danger. The *puntillero* pulled out his dagger and finished off the slaughter.

The trumpets blared. The bells rang gaily, and three mules arrived at a trot. The slaughtered bull was tied behind them and dragged out of the arena. I had no time to recover from the bloody spectacle and catch my breath: without a break, the gate opened again, and out stepped the second bull. This one was white with black patches, and slender. Its horns were sharp as swords.

Once again the formalities began. At first the bull snorted calmly, happily, as though it were frolicking in a meadow. I shall never forget its sweet disposition and strength and innocence. But suddenly the *picadores* sprang. The *matador* came. In a lightning-flash, the sword was stuck through its throat, had pierced its heart. All the spectators leaped up, screaming with joy. A woman near me was laughing. Her eyes rolled. They had a dazed, erotic expression. The bullock staggered, struggling to stand up. But its legs were trembling, shifting about. It collapsed and groveled in the sand. It was a horrifying, indescribable dance. It must have lasted only a few seconds, but these two or three seconds made me feel the meaning of eternity. The bull danced, knelt down, got up again, couldn't even bellow, then suddenly, all at once, collapsed on the ground dead.

The third bull was a marvel of beauty and strength. Colored like a bee, plump, with piercing horns. As it came in, it smelled the blood on the sand and understood the killing. Its damp nostrils twitched angrily, and its red eyes whirled. Suddenly it caught sight of the horseman in the shade, and charged him with a bellow. The lance missed its mark and the horseman fell off his horse. Furious, the bull sank its horns into the horse's belly. The belly opened, and the horse's entrails and guts dangled on the ground. The horse neighed in terrible pain, kicking at its own guts till its legs got tangled in them and they gushed out on the sand. The *banderillos* ran into the arena, but retreated in terror over the wooden fence, with the bull in pursuit. Then the bull also jumped over the planks. The spectators let out a hushed cry of terror. But the beast was driven back and the boards were nailed in place again.

Now the *matador* emerged, his sword concealed behind the red cape. They stood again face to face: the man and the bull-god. They touched each other's extremities, as though caressing each other. A moment of jubilation, for the grand reconciliation seemed to have come. Bloodless and peaceful, the great meeting would now take place. God and man would be fused by love . . . no longer killing. But suddenly, the matador's sword blade flashed between the bull's straight horns. The bullfighter began to cower, drawing back his sword. The angry public heckled him and he felt ashamed of himself. He unsheathed his sword again, took aim, and struck. But again he missed his mark. He could not pierce straight through the heart, and the sword remained stuck between the horns. Shaking its head desperately, the beast flung the sword aside, and, raging mad, wheeled on its tormentor, who by now had been handed another sword. For several seconds, they both stood absolutely still, face to face. At that instant, I was aware of the magnificent quality of the human being: slender, delicately built, lightly dressed as if on his way to a dance; his high forehead shone calmly in the shade. Confronting him, puffing violently, the dark force of the animal —the animal and the god.

I could hear all the hearts of the people around me beating in harmony. The same worship was uniting them all: the worship of the bull. The same cry rose from deep inside all of us: Ah, ah, if we could but touch its shiny skin; hang upon its sword-sharp horns; feel the blood of the bull lapping through our own veins; and so become one with its heartbeat! But since none of us here was capable of wrestling with this divine force, we had sent our representative—the most initiated, the most familiar with the sacred bull—to fight it and play with it. To represent all the devotees, and become fused with the bull in an eternal way: by killing it. Here, killing is the outcome of an unbearable love. The sacred marriage and the sacred killing are identical. This identity must seem mad to delicate, naïve souls. But anyone who has genuinely loved will understand it. Blood, the uniting with blood, the immortalization of Love by means of Death, are profound human necessities. Only nowadays, civilization has obscured them and made them mute. Here suddenly at the extreme edge of the Mediterranean, they come back to life in a most simple and mysterious way.

By the time I left, night had already fallen. I was aware of some unexpected mystic power inside me: as though I had communed with and gained a part of the bull's power. I felt a grave serenity, an austere joy. The horrendous struggle was followed by a reconciliation within myself between life and man; man and God; God and death.

The shores of Spain are disappearing behind me. Along the far horizon of the sea, outlined against the sky, the airy, graceful, steep mountain ranges still roll on.

Once again, my beloved Mediterranean is cooling my burning brow. I close my eyes, and in my imagination, the whole turbulent, kaleidoscopic, crowded vision of Spain wells up. I am trying to make my memory array clearly these treasures from this new pirate trip of my spirit. I want to preserve them with mathematical precision inside myself: the Alhambra; the mosque at Cordova; the great Cathedral at Burgos; the women with jasmine in their hair; the orange groves of Valencia; the slender flames of El Greco and the pitiless, terrifying visions of Goya. . . . A woman flashing for a moment on a balcony in Cordova, then swiftly disappearing; a full moon on an August night on a great street in Madrid; the first warm rainfalls beneath the ripe date trees in Aligada. And from one end of Spain to the other, stretching like a red battlefront: thick drops of blood; bitter thoughts; keen fleeting joys; laughter; tears. And above all else, that last day of mine in Spain: the shiny bull; the woman laughing; the sword stuck between the horns; the man who killed the god so that he might become one with him.

I had also sensed it earlier. But that day, my heart was profoundly shaken, for now it was certain: life is a mortal struggle of love and death; a terrifying, hopeless, lionhearted adventure of Don Quixote.

And here was the finest trophy of this Spanish campaign.

DON QUIXOTE

■ DON QUIXOTE*

His mind fumed and all boundaries grew dim,
imagination licked the world about him
and roaring, rearing fires clothed him round.

Then, like a salamander, Fate drew near
and licked her lips amid the cooling flames;
his mind leapt high in the barren wilderness

and as his still unerring black eyes blazed,
behold, in the far distant fields he saw
Faith passing by, suckling the miracle;

and like the Virgin Mary was her sweetness.
His soul rushed off to hide in its own dream,
for it still choked on earth, shouting for freedom—

and then that flaming, feudal lord of wastes,
that great and gaunt ascetic, Don Quixote,
reared stiffly straight and suffered in her groans.

"Be still, my soul," that ancient archon cried;
"whatever God has left half finished here,
I, as his warrior, shall complete it now!"

---

* Translated from the Greek by Kimon Friar.

149

Then in the highest summit of desire
his burning eyes stood still to spy the land—
help them, dear God, to burn unceasingly.

O pitiless wasteland, the Last Judgment's hour—
here without water, without bird or hope,
and all Creation a black skein of snakes.

"Dear God, I've never seen such poison before,"
the pallid lips sang out with trembling fear,
"nor such a merciless and sterile country;

I see I must have taken God's road indeed."
He closed his eyes and his whole body shook;
on his left shoulder blade a small bird hopped

and with erotic yearning temptingly
sang the great sweetness of the other world:
"A cool house of my own that whitely gleams

by the sea's azure edge, a brimming sweetness
deep in my heart, and by the holy hearth
a buxom woman suckling my own son."

This is no bird, this is no nightingale!
O heart, do not be fooled, do not turn back,
for look, our Lady Freedom now approaches."

His scraggly horse then by the sudden edge
of the abyss neighed loud and opened its lips:
"Alas, where are you going, master? Take pity

on the poor flesh, for soon the sun will set.
Ah, let's return at once to that cool stable,
the earth, filled with most fresh and most sweet clo

Thus did the body speak, that sluggish seed
on the tall tree of God, and downward shook
with fear and trembling its long horsy head,

but still its master listened to his heart:
"This is the nature of Idea's kingdom;
its benefactions are those poisonous snakes

and but one curly flower—the subtle scent
and secret fragrance of our only love,
our nonexistent Lady, Dulcinea.

And as we roam our whole life long, we'll trace
our dear beloved's footprints on all roads;
and when we thirst, we'll have but our own blood

to lick on stones, like any common dog,
and but one lone companion on our way,
our faithful, stalking lion, ravening Death.

Forward! Without a single hope, but even
as though the eyes will one day see all that
they long to see, fight on, O gallant knight!

This, father, be your greatest pride: that you
have taken windmills for high castle walls
and fight with threatening shadows in mid-air.

The icy stars above you will laugh long,
and men below will shout derision at all
you do, but you, with the seducing joy

of most ferocious freedom and of death
will sweetly smile, O greatly martyred soul,
and leave drops of your rich blood everywhere.

Bound firmly still to virtue's rigid mast,
you shall pass on with your thin arms outspread,
and all the swallows of March shall swoop in flocks

to build their nests within those hollow pits
your soul has eaten in your holy body,
and in your armpits, shoulders and tall throat.

And you, in the divine lie fortified—
that resurrection still exists—shall paint
the eggs of springtime with your holy blood.

But you were nourished on rich marrow bone
and scattered your grain lavishly, like chaff;
you turned then to that hunting hound, your heart,

untied the thongs of the unvalorous mind
till in the vineyards of the imagination,
with bows and arrows made of swift light rays,

amid a shower of stones, guffaws and laughter,
we, too, with battered armor rushed to hunt
that most exotic peacock, our own dream.

What joy! Tall mountain summits! On these heights
our brows are beaten by the purest winds,
for we've escaped at last all loathsome breaths

and broken at last the tight reins of prudence.
What is most difficult in all creation?
That's what our own heart wants, and does not tremble.

Out of our tangled entrails' darkest woods
let's bring to light all justice, kindness, joy,
all those wild birds that built their far nests there,

and though they never appear, may that hot kiln
of the inner earth burn on unceasingly!
Feed the full flames yourself, until injustice,

shameless intoxication and poverty
shall turn into pure gold and Don Quixote.
Earth and all life shall take on nobleness,

the flower of youth shall blossom deathlessly,
for that unerring archer, man's pure mind,
loves only the quarry that's unattainable.

Ah father, I know it well: deep in your entrails
all pain lies coiled like a dread snake. Lock up
your groans within your heart, even though they choke you,

for never forget, O Hopeless Man, that you
are still the greatest hope of widowed earth.
Shake now your widespread and sungolden wings

until the earth, that scurfy old peahen,
shall turn to a proud peacock sauntering
in the sun's brilliant warmth and golden rays.

You are the youngest, favorite son of God,
his dearest treasure and his purest gold,
his ultimate bastion: firm, impregnable;

for the Old Master at long last has hung
his highest hopes on your tall crimson plume
and on your splintered, your most foolish spear.

You are his only worthy champion! Rise,
and from man's foul condition snatch your God;
arm yourself not with earth, but rearing flames

and a long wing for trowel that your divine
insanity and nonchalance may push you on.
Rise, warrior, and begin the Second Creation!"

Thus did the heart lament and laugh together,
and as the mighty athlete stooped above
his wretched saddle, listening to the new

small voice, behold a tiny goldfinch hopped
on his head's dome, raised its firm neck erect
and crimson-throated burst in flaming song.

O how the breast and wings of that bird quivered!
until from too much warbling one small drop
of blood hung from its yellow beak, and trembled.

Then earth, our gray-haired mother, leapt and turned
into a huge goldfinch, throat erect in sun,
that beat its now enormous wings and burst

into a new tune never before heard on earth.
Soon on desire's highest branch, the siren
of all deeds unattainable arose,

and in her hand held murder like a wreath.
Deeply within that untamed virgin's eyes
our ancient archon gazed and there beheld

loneliness, poverty and pain, and not
a single man approached the loved one's breast.
Captain Sole bit his lips till the blood ran.

All life now, like a long complaining myth,
wrapped itself round the swift reel of his mind
until he started off from God's dark depths,

and, floundering in the tight nets of his dream,
entered into his Lady's kingdom thus.
Above his head the deep and starry sky

shed all its leaves and broke in lamentation;
but he in silence spurred his wretched nag,
and slowly, of all strength exhausted, took

the hopeless, long ascension of his soul.

pART ii:

viva La muerte!

■ VIVA LA MUERTE!—

[AUTHOR'S NOTE]

■ ONE OF THE brightest faces on earth, the face of Spain, is dark now. Airplanes pass over her like birds of prey. Smoke and fires rise over her. A piercing cry convulses Castile, Andalusia, Estremadura, Catalonia, that rends the human heart. Cities and villages fall in ruins. Men, women, children take arms and kill each other. Toledo stands in ruins. Immortal now in legend, like Missolonghi, Madrid, once a charming, carefree, voluptuous princess, is in flames.

The news from beyond the Pyrenees is muffled and contradictory—of bestial and heroic acts; fiery words; overweening cruel deeds; men burned alive; graves opened; unending rows of human lives pinned against the walls and shot down. The age-old hatred of brother for brother has erupted unmercifully. The terrifying modern ideas have collided fatally and are annihilating humanity.

The whole world is standing around this new inhuman arena of the bullfight, listening, holding its breath. No one is a mere spectator. No one is base enough to feel indifferent as they listen and watch. Everyone is grieving for the grief of Spain. For deep down, the grief of Spain is also our own grief, the grief of every individual and every people. We are all profoundly aware that the character of Spanish history, which has brought the two opponents face to face, is also the character of our own history. The Spanish war, in its deeper essence, is not a civil war. It is international.

That is why anyone who goes to Spain today has a great

159

responsibility, if he decides to report her fearful tragedy to other human beings. He is no longer out of danger. He can no longer be irresponsible, free to portray costumes, landscapes, gardens and old churches and pretty scenes, or exotic spectacles: the gypsies of Seville, the dancers and the castanets and the bullfights. None of this is seen by the traveler nowadays. It has all vanished. The spectacles he witnesses are different. Now his evidence is fraught with responsibility. Its value is as an historical document and a contribution to humanity. Lies, exaggeration, vain lyricism—all the paraphernalia of the other mood—are inappropriate in the presence of such human suffering.

I went and saw. My eyes filled. I talked with the leaders, lived with the soldiers, entered ruined villages, listened to the laments of women mourning their dead, climbed over corpses killed in the war, read letters found in their pockets, followed battles on dry land and in the air, watched from the banks of the Manzanares as Madrid was being consumed.

This war has an ineffably tragic quality, for all these people who are killing one another are victims of the needs of our transitional age. They are not cold-hearted or cowardly. They are all warm-blooded Africans—a rich, complex, fierce race: Spaniards. Behind their temporary masks, whether red or black, the naked face of the Spaniard is always there, full of passion and fire. A few years ago, we had seen this fiery face at the bullfights. Thousands of men and women passionately intent on the combat: the agony and death of the bull. Nowadays we are present at a similar combat, except that now it is between man and man, no longer bull and man. No longer bullfights, but manfights. The primeval mysterious intoxication aroused by the blood; the return to the roots of man and beast; the sudden rending of the airy cloak that is embroidered with such artistry and goes by the name of Civilization; the revelation that at the bottom of every great and critical human action lies not economic or moral self-interest, but Passion—by which we mean a pre-human tempestuous force that is beyond logic and self-interest.

At these critical moments, life is not the supreme good. This point will throw light on, explain many things in the present unprecedented and savage drama of Spain. At such moments as these, we regret not having ten or twenty lives to light and burn them all. They who sit serenely at home or spend their time in passionate discussions in the cafés are terrified of bloodshed. They read what is happening in Spain and shudder. They see photographs and catch their breath. But the others, who take an active part in the historical movement, feel a wild excitement. Immersed in the warm blood, they become intoxicated; feel an overpowering giddiness; an animal pleasure that is eternal and human. At the portals of death, they experience joys that are incomprehensible to the others who just sit and think.

Now that I am setting about writing, I am aware of the full responsibility of my evidence. I shall tell all that I saw honestly, clearly, impartially. Because my purpose, conscious or subconscious, is not to support this or that idea; is not to cover up or praise the heroic acts or crimes of this or that camp. My purpose lies elsewhere: to offer the evidence for everything I saw and heard, and so lay bare to you this gaping human wound that goes by the name of Spain today. Perhaps tomorrow, it will be called France or the whole world. . . .

During this critical moment Spain is passing (and with her, all humanity), I find myself at a point of the battle where I am vulnerable to darts from both camps. After a violent and painful struggle inside myself, I chose this position of mine of my own free will. Not with any stupid or supercilious intention; not because of being indifferent to the darts. But because I believe that nowadays, the most difficult and beneficial duty of the thinking man is to tell the truth. Of necessity, this truth is bitter and disagreeable to all the combatants. But that does not matter. One day it will be of use in creating the future.

I shall not hide anything. We are passing a diabolical bend of History. It goes by a multitude of names: hate; war; prehistoric darkness; chaos. But if we can see clearly and fight honestly, perhaps at the end, the following name will survive, dipped in blood as is always the case in History: the New Civilization. I shall relate everything I saw and heard, without crystallizing any opinion of my own. What good could a personal opinion do in the face of this present fatal clash that is driving men, regimenting them, killing them without mercy. Such an opinion would be superficial and absurd: like going to watch a horrendous earthquake to judge and take sides in it: accusing the dark forces of Nature for having rent the crust of the earth and swallowed up her cities.

On the boat I took to Portugal, before crossing over to Spanish soil, there was a German philosopher, Dr. Colin Rose. He too was on his way to Spain and happened to be in the same cabin with me. He asked me:

"Are you for or against the war?"

"Neither for nor against," was my answer. "As I am neither for nor against an earthquake."

In Palma on the island of Majorca, where I first debarked on my way to Spain, I sensed tremendous ferment. Soldiers, civilians, angry women, young girls decked out in all their finery, old men leaning on their tall sticks—all of them massed in front of the barracks, reading the news bulletins posted on the walls. It was raining. Big cannon glistened gaily, seeming to laugh in the rain. The great Gothic Cathedral of Palma was thronged with pigeons that had taken refuge from the rain beneath its doors. They were perched on the saints' heads or nestled under the marble wings of the angels. The whole cathedral was full of cooing sounds, like a female pigeon's love-call. Just then, a little boat was taking off. It was crammed with soldiers, and then another, laden with the same tragic cargo. Hands were raised in the fascist salute. Handkerchiefs waved. Hurrahs were heard:

"*Viva la Muerte!* Long live Death!"

Then, out of a corner of the cathedral, emerged a girl about fifteen years old, wearing a red and yellow head scarf (the national colors) on her curly head:

"Pst! Pst!" she whispered, calling to a little soldier who was getting ready to jump into the second boat.

The little soldier (he couldn't have been more than fifteen years old) laughed, ran back, grabbed the girl by the waist, squeezed himself under the arched door of the cathedral. They spoke the eternal human words . . . the war disappeared. Their two faces shone, enveloped in the calm warm rain of Majorca.

And then it was that I sensed how war intensifies to the highest pitch all the griefs and joys of man. A single tiny detail may give the keenest pleasure to someone involved in the war—such as cannot be felt by someone else who is out of danger, who just sits leisurely thinking about the war. The real meaning of a woman, wine, sun, a flower—their incalculable preciousness—can only be sensed by someone who is on his way to death. And that is why I was not surprised by the spectacle enacted before me from the moment I set foot on Spanish soil: blithe gaiety, high spirits, the noisy hubbub of a festival—a psychology identical with the psychology of the public at the bullfights. The fierce atmosphere of the wrestling arena, the stage scenery of a popular theater—thick paint, lively colors, picturesque costumes of rags and velvet—women, children, men chewing sesame-seeds, reading newspapers, smoking, coming and going to the tune of loud discussions, in the corridors of the bloodstained theater be tween Burgos and Salamanca; between Toledo and Seville; between Barcelona and Valencia; Bilbao; Málaga; and Madrid. . . .

N.K., Autumn, 1936

■ CÁCERES

■ WE WERE CROSSING the borders of Portugal, coming into the sparse olive groves and gray rocks and autumn scarlet vineyards of Estremadura. Treeless villages carved out of granite. Yellow corn and red peppers hanging in bunches over the doors.

I was squeezed into a train compartment full of soldiers. Everyone's knees jostling the next man's. They were using a cardboard suitcase as a tabletop. Each one opened his knapsack as fast as he could: tins of sardines; bread as white as lime; black olives; huge abundant red peppers. They began to eat. A small leather flask, the *bota*, was passed around from mouth to mouth. They pressed it, till the wine bubbled up through a small hole and made a clicking sound in their mouths. They were in a good mood, and started singing the hymn of the Falange.

A plump, gay little soldier could no longer restrain his enthusiasm. He threw his arms up in the air and cried:

"*Viva la Muerte!* Long live Death!"

Again the *bota* was passed from mouth to mouth. Through the window harsh gray granite stones came into sight, and the silver olive trees and red vineyards. Here and there, a little house made of sunbaked stone.

A slender young man, wounded in the throat, couldn't tilt his head back to take a drink. So they moved his head for him, wedging the flask in between his lips till he could get a

swig. He had been at the Alcázar, one of the "Free Besieged."
I questioned him, but he refused to talk about anything.

"I don't want to talk!" he shouted in a hoarse voice. "I
don't want to! What good are words? Take a look at me here
. . . I used to be fat as a barrel! And I lost forty pounds."

They all burst out laughing and took another swig, then
tilted the hero's head again, till his mouth was full of wine.
As he swallowed it, he gulped with pain:

"I lost forty pounds!" he repeated, wiping his lips. "Forty
pounds! That's what the Alcázar means! Just that!"

Now our train was moving along wild lonely mountains.
A shepherd dressed in a huge black cape waved from the
rocks, calling to us:

"*Diario, diario!* Newspaper!"

They threw him a newspaper, and his dog ran out to catch
it.

A fortress rose in front of us against the noonday sky.
Houses, flags, all sorts of caps, balconies covered with bright
yellow blankets and white sheets and red crosses. We had arrived in the capital city of Estremadura: Cáceres. The sun
was glaring with its direct noonday light. On a white sheet
there was a big red heart embroidered: the heart of Christ
pierced with a spear. Large inscriptions on the walls and over
the gates, proclaiming: "Long live Spain! Long live Christ!"
Moroccans, dressed in jelab capes and turbans; women, heavily painted with mascara and powders; buxom nurses with
big red crosses on their full bosoms, rushing to and fro, greeting the soldiers, strutting by with swaying movements, then
on their way back calling out "*Arriba España!*" as they wet
their lips.

"What's going on?" I asked a little old woman standing in
her doorway with her hands folded, calmly surveying the
scene.

"Nothing, my child. Nothing . . . just war."

In a little garden, the women and children were sitting on benches, chewing sesame seeds. A group of ten young men in red caps marched past.

"Who are these?" I asked an old man.

The old man swallowed his sesame seeds quickly, and answered:

"*Requetes.*"

"What's that?"

"Well, they want to bring back the king. Can't you hear what they're shouting? *Rey, rey, O! Rey, rey, O!*"

"You're not wearing a red cap," I said to the old man. "So that means you're a democrat?"

"I'm not wearing one 'cause they didn't give me one. It's made of pure wool, and now winter's coming on soon."

He laughed and looked toward the public square. It was flooded with soldiers, all wearing different caps. He shook his head, spat and remarked:

"All these are Spanish heads. Don't look at their caps, *caballero!* Don't look at their caps!"

Medieval stone balconies before me; towers, fortress gates, palaces, suns carved on the lintels of the houses, stars, panoplies, strange wild beasts. The women smile at the soldiers. Their heavy stare lingers on them sadly and tenderly. The mood of the whole city is like an army camp. Love and death are fusing again, deceiving men and women with sudden, strange bursts of joy. The men seem to have acquired new rights, seem to have taken courage. "Give me a kiss," their new song goes. For many nights now, I haven't been able to sleep, because of this song. "Give me a kiss, for I'm on my way to war." In the women, the age-old instincts of sexual and maternal love are aroused, as well as compassion. "He's

on his way to war. . . . He's on his way to war," each of
them muses with overwhelming tenderness. The women
seem to feel they owe these men in the shadow of death this
cruelest pleasure, known as love. They no longer have the
courage to refuse them. They must now fulfill their eternal
obligation.

I felt exhilarated as I inhaled this fiery air, wending my
way into the ancient narrow streets of Cáceres. From here
the clatter and noise of the public square could not be heard.
Life recovered its own peaceful rhythm. Donkeys, laden with
cantaloupe melons and watermelons and grapes, ambled to
and fro. Women carried shiny water jugs erect on top of their
heads.

I stopped in front of a small house. The door was wide
open, and I looked inside. The black slates on the floor were
freshly scrubbed. There was a water jug in the corner; two
sparkling clean towels, a fireplace in the background. In the
very front, three old ladies were sitting in a semicircle,
dressed all in black, tightly veiled in their mantillas. Opposite
them sat an old man with a white beard all prickly like a
brush. All of them were stooped over, listening mutely to a
young woman, who stood chattering in the doorway. She was
talking on and on, gesturing continuously, as she told them
about a chicken she'd lost. How she'd run back and forth,
and hadn't been able to find it anywhere, and now look!
She'd finally found it sitting calmly in the kitchen, laying
eggs. She was talking feverishly as she described this amazing
event to the four old characters. As for them, they just listened in silence, still stooped over the ground, like characters
from an ancient tragedy: the two choruses and the messenger.
Life without change; the eternal themes; the immortal, everyday routine. . . .

Now I went back to the heart of the feverish excitement:

the public square. On my way, I passed a big fountain decorated with shiny yellow and eggplant-colored slabs. It glistened all over, underneath the enormous arched gate. There
was a crowd of young girls there, filling their water jugs.
They were yelling and cackling. The soldiers crowded around
and began teasing them, making gestures and remarks in
their own army vernacular. And the girls cackled, as though
someone was tickling them. I stopped a moment, enchanted.
A little soldier, sporting a yellow tassel, turned around. He
was holding a buxom girl in his arms.

"Foreigner?" he asked me, without letting go of the girl.
"*Alemán?*"

"What're you doing there?" I asked him with a laugh.

"Ah, ah . . ." the soldier answered, as though he were
trying to sum up the great blessings of life: "*Mujer y sangre!*
Woman and blood!"

An old man, who was also waiting to fill up his water jug,
added wistfully:

"*Y tabaco!* And tobacco!"

Ten members of the Falange passed by, their arms linked,
shoulder to shoulder, singing the hymn of the Falange. In
front of them marched two young women of the Falange
wearing the five red arrows of the Falange embroidered over
their hearts, and holding themselves erect, their chests protruding. I cocked my ear to listen. The way these strong
young throats sang their hymn, it reverberated far beyond
the borders of Spain; reverberated beyond the Idea it
hymned, and with slight changes, turned into an international hymn of love and death:

> *Facing the sun with a new shirt*
> *that you stitched yesterday in red,*
> *I shall find death, if she seeks me,*

and shall never see you again.
I shall line up by my comrades
who guard the morning stars
with an impassive gesture that
runs through our very eagerness.
If they tell you that I fell,
it will be in the front lines.
Flags will come back with victory,
with the happy tread of peace,
and be adorned with five roses,
arrows of my brigade.
Now waiting in sky, land and sea,
spring will come and laugh again.
March on, brigades, to victory!
For light is dawning over Spain. *

I was tired and fell asleep. That night seemed to me like a single condensed moment, distilled in honey. It rested my body, made my brain feel tranquil, renewing the mysterious human mechanism so that it could face all the burdens of the coming day without collapsing.

---

* Translated by Willis Barnstone.

■ SALAMANCA

■ It is noon, and I am wandering around the
streets of Salamanca. Cathedral, university; medieval palaces,
princely balconies, unselfish pleasures, Art—that plaything of
the free man—have all vanished, giving way to the fiery
atmosphere of war. Now the cars race at a crazy speed. There
are sentries on every street corner, national flags and drums,
officers pacing up and down in the ancient palace of the
Archbishop. And there, invisible, never sleeping, the stubborn taciturn Franco is now steering the destiny of the New
Spain.

We are living a great legend which is still warm with bloodshed and fire. I am sitting in Franco's antechamber, waiting
to get the *salvoconducto* that will allow me to circulate freely.
I look around me avidly. Priests dressed in black satin cassocks are gliding past noiselessly. They have thick eyebrows,
are freshly shaven, refined, silent, wreathed in smiles. Their
whole bodies seem to smile. They are sure of success. Their
roots go deep. Several thousands of them have been killed,
and with this increase in the number of the martyrs, the
Church's coat of arms has been refurbished. Religion has
once again become involved in the intense self-interests of
present-day life here. Once again it has entered the battlefield of modern life. Today the Spanish Church is no longer
a mere tradition decked in ancient parchments. It has become a beloved personality. With its many wounds, it now

moves at ease in corridors, where generals move. When it returns among its own friends, it proudly displays its new
wounds.

The music floats into the courtyard underneath Franco's
high windows. The people are assembling in the streets.
Women, with heavy make-up and fresh hairdos, step forward
expectantly. Nothing is missing: priests, soldiers, women,
music, multi-colored caps, an invisible leader working high
above them behind a heavy curtain. Nothing missing! And
the Spaniards are happy that their life has a new color and
significance.

The director of Franco's diplomatic staff approaches me.
He is a young man with fine features and eyes exhausted
from lack of sleep. He is bringing me the *salvoconducto*, with
Franco's signature.

"Where do you want to go first?" he asks me.

"Toledo."

The young man's eyes light up:

"I shall never forget the scene that day we entered Toledo
and freed the heroes of the Alcázar. We saw strange creatures
emerging out of the fortress catacombs. They made us shudder—ghosts, they were. All the men had beards. All of them
—men and women alike—had grown skeleton-thin. They
seemed tremendously tall to us. Their eyes were enormous,
overshadowing their whole face. Then, for the first time, I
understood El Greco. I realized from what deep regions of
his mind, and what painful yearning, El Greco had brought
his heroes forth into the light."

I didn't want to leave Salamanca without seeing the terrifying old porcupine, Unamuno. While I was waiting till it was
time to knock on his door, I walked back and forth in the

autumnal garden outside the church of Santa María de los Caballeros. The leaves had turned yellow. The poplars were glistening all gold. Three huge motionless cypresses that never change, regardless of spring or winter, stood dark black against the vermilion evening light. In my mind, I had crystallized two major questions that I wanted to put to Unamuno:

—Nowadays, what is the duty of the man of the spirit? Is his duty to take part in the struggle? And if so, with whom?

—How do you feel about the present moment in Spain and in the world? The new war is on its way; indeed, has already arrived. In Spain, the first skirmish is already taking place. Can we (and ought we to) prevent it?

I knocked on his door and entered a rectangular office. There were very few books, two big tables, two romantic landscapes on the walls, large windows, abundant light, an English book lying open on the desk. I cocked my ear. From far down the corridor, I could hear Unamuno's footsteps coming closer. They sounded tired, shuffling, like an old man's step. Where were the great strides and youthful resilience I had so admired in him, only several years ago in Madrid?

When the door opened, I saw that all of a sudden, Unamuno had aged. He had faded away. He was hunched over. But his eyes still flashed. They were still eternally awake: quick, violent like a bullfighter's. I didn't have time to open my mouth before Unamuno rushed impetuously into the center of the ring:

"I'm in despair!" he cried, clenching his fists. "Despair at what's going on here! The way they're fighting, killing each other, burning the churches, making ceremonies, raising the Red flags and the standards of Christ. You think all this is happening because the Spaniards have faith? With half of them believing in the religion of Christ, and the other half in Lenin's religion! No! Not a bit of it! Listen. Pay close attention to what I'm going to say to you: All these things are happening because the Spaniards don't believe in anything! Nothing. . . . Nothing! They are *desperados*. No other language in the world has this word. Because no other nation except Spain has what it stands for. *Desperado* means the man who knows perfectly well that he has nothing to hold on to; who believes in nothing; and since he does not believe, is governed by a wild rage."

Then Unamuno was silent for a moment, staring out his window.

"How are you getting on in Greece?" he asked. But without waiting for an answer, he plunged back into the ring:

"The Spanish people have gone mad!" he exclaimed. "Not only the Spanish people; the whole world today. And why? Because the standard of young people all over the world has suffered a spiritual collapse. They not only scorn the Spirit. They hate it. They hate the Spirit. Yes, that's what stamps all the young people in the world nowadays. They want sports, action, war, the class struggle. Why do you think they want these things? . . . Because they hate the Spirit. We are told they want to base themselves on reality. They despise, so we are told, romantic daydreams, sentimentality, abstract ideas. And why do you think they despise them? . . . Because they hate the Spirit. Oh, I know these young people of today very well, these modernists! They hate the Spirit!"

He got up and went over to look for the English book that lay open on his desk. He found a phrase and read it.

"You see?" he said. "They hate the Spirit!"

Just at that moment, I rushed to get a question in edgewise:

"Well, what are the people who still love the Spirit supposed to do?"

Unamuno did a rare thing: he listened. He remained silent awhile, and then suddenly burst out again:

"Nothing!" he roared. "Nothing! The face of the truth is terrifying. What is our duty? To hide the truth from the people! The Old Testament says: 'He who looks God in the face will die.' Even Moses could not look God straight in the face. He looked at Him from behind and saw only an edge of His robe. Such is the nature of the truth! We must deceive the people; deceive them, so that the poor creatures can have the strength and cheerfulness to go on living. If they knew the truth, they couldn't go on. They wouldn't want to live any more. The people need myth, illusion, deception. These are what support their lives. Here, I've written a book on this awful theme—my last book. Take it."

He'd regained his old vigor. His veins overflowed with blood again. His cheeks were flushed and his body was erect. He seemed rejuvenated. In one great stride, he reached his bookshelf and took down a book. Hastily he jotted down a few words in it and handed it to me.

"Take it. *The Martyr San Manuel Bueno.* Read it. You'll see. My hero is a Catholic priest who does not believe. But he is struggling to give his people the faith which he himself lacks, and in that way, to give them the strength to live. To live! For he knows that without faith, without hope, the people cannot go on living."

He laughed a sarcastic, despairing laugh:

"For fifty years now, I haven't been to confession. But I've given confession to priests, monks, nuns. I'm not interested in the clerics who eat and drink heavily or hoard money. I'm more interested in the ones who love women. They're the ones who really suffer. And the ones who have ceased believing interest me even more. The tragedy of these people is terrifying. Such is the hero of my book, San Manuel Bueno. Take a look!"

Unamuno's violent hand began skimming through the book.

"The truth is something terrifying, unbearable, lethal. If simple people learn it, they will no longer be able to go on living. And they must live. . . . They must live!"

Unamuno tore through the pages in great haste, and began to read. He read on and on. He seemed madly excited at hearing his own words and his own voice. He read the whole book, then stopped:

"Well, what do you say?" he asked me. "What's your opinion?"

"As at the end of Greco-Roman civilization," was my answer, "so today, the dialectical mind has gone too far and is no longer helpful for life. We no longer believe in myth, and for that reason our life is barren. I think the time has come for the dialectical mind to fall into a deep sleep—to sleep so that the deep creative powers of man can awaken."

"So you mean a kind of new Middle Ages?" Unamuno exclaimed, and his eyes were full of fire. "I've said the same thing: I said one day to Valéry: 'The mind cannot digest the great progress it has made. It must rest.'"

At that instant, music sounded underneath his windows, and uproar and soldiers hurrahing: "Long live Spain! *Arriba España!*" Unamuno listened intently. The uproar passed. And once again, the voice of the old man of Spain was heard, exhausted now and sad:

"At this critical moment of Spain's suffering, I know I should go with the soldiers. They're the ones who will bring order. They know what discipline means, and know how to impose it. I have not become a rightist. Don't pay any atten-

tion to what people say. I haven't betrayed the cause of freedom. It's just that, for the time being, it was absolutely essential that order be imposed. But one day soon, I'll rise again
and plunge back into the struggle for freedom, all alone. I
am no fascist, or a Bolshevik either—I am alone!"

I was trying to turn the conversation, for I could see the
great suffering of the snowy-haired gladiator. But the Old Man
would not let me.

"I am alone!" he roared once more, and got up. "Alone,
like Croce in Italy!"

When I left, night had fallen, and I was softly murmuring
the verses of Antonio Machado on this violent, anarchic
desperado of a fighter.

> *This donquixotic*
> *don Miguel de Unamuno, a rugged Basque,*
> *wears the grotesque armor*
> *and absurd helmet*
> *of a good Manchegan. Don Miguel goes about*
> *as a rider on a monstrous steed*
> *jabbing gold spurs wildly;*
> *wholly deaf to gossiping tongues.*
>
> *To the drovers of his country,*
> *the bill collectors, gamblers, profiteers,*
> *he preaches lessons of chivalry,*
> *and some day he may wake the vapid*
> *soul of his people that is still asleep,*
> *despite the clamor of his iron mace.*
>
> *He wants to show the knight a frown*
> *of doubt before he gallops off,*

and like a new Hamlet he would stare
at the naked blade near his heart.

He has the vigor of a rugged breed
who made a big splash abroad,
who sought gold beyond the seas.
He wants to be a founder, and says, "I believe:
up with God and the Spanish mind!" *

---

* Translated from the Spanish by Willis Barnstone.

■ VARGAS

■ I LEFT SALAMANCA and Unamuno behind me, hurrying on to reach Toledo. Olive groves, vineyards, tiny oaks denuded of their bark. Here and there a house half in ruins; a woman washing, cooking, removing the lice from her children. From far off, the sounds of cannon. We were getting closer to the front. The fields were rifled with holes. Pieces of bombs, bullet shells, Communist newspapers, letters thrown out on the roads, photographs, a tattered Red flag. . . .

We were coming down into the town of Vargas. There were about fifty men of the Guardia Civil traveling with me. We were all on our way to Toledo. At the entrance to the village, the women flew out at us. They ran ahead, pointing to the ruined walls and broken locks and skeletons of houses. The wind was blowing and the hinges of the doors began to squeak. They sounded like wailing. I went in and out of house after house. Everywhere piles of rags, the remains of mattresses, sheets, linen. There were still photographs hanging on the walls of laughing children and newlyweds clasping each other's hands.

A few of the village girls had stayed behind with their old parents. When they learned that fifty Guardia Civil had made their appearance, they fixed the spitcurls or *tagos* on their foreheads and temples as fast as they could, then began strolling up and down the deserted square. They were chattering in shrill voices and laughing for the soldiers to hear them. They did hear them, and jumped up from the one wine shop still left with its one small cask of wine. They formed a circle around the girls. The ruined village was transformed. The dead were forgotten. On the cheap black blouses, a red rose blazed.

Man's soul has a cruel power of forgetfulness. Almost the whole village had been washed away: fathers, brothers, fiancés, husbands—they'd all gone into the ground. Their corpses were still fresh. The girls had struck up the funeral lament. Anyone who'd heard them during those first days would have said: "They'll never be happy again. Their life is finished!" How many days had passed? And suddenly here over the bloodstained roads, fifty uniformed men had appeared. And the girls twined ribbons in their hair, moistened and bit their lips to make them red and came out for a stroll. "*Arriba España!*" The soldiers shouted the fascist greeting as they approached. The girls laughed. They knew this patriotic cry was a transparent mask, and behind the mask, the tiny face of Cupid was clearly visible, shining tenderly like a little child, but devilishly.

Little by little, the Guardia Civil, with their shiny three-cornered hats and guns, and the young girls with their hook-shaped curls and voluptuous breasts, began strolling out beyond the village. They reached the threshing mills, which were still strewn with unsorted hay.

Meanwhile, up in the little tower of the Town Hall, two workmen were unscrewing a plaque engraved in big gold letters: "Democracy Square." They were perched up on a wall to take it down; laughing away, as if they were tearing down Democracy with their own hands.

"What're you going to put up there now?" I asked them.

"What you say?"

"What're you going to put there in its place? . . . Alfonso? . . . Franco? . . . The Virgin Mary?"

"We don't know yet," the workmen answered, working furiously to get it down. "They haven't brought us the new one yet!"

But all things have their natural end, both war and love. A trumpet player climbed up to the Town Hall tower and blew the call to action on his trumpet. A fine dust had risen from the straw. The Guardia Civil brushed themselves off, straightened their three-cornered hats and took off. They reached the trucks, and we all crowded in. The patriotic songs began. We were moving on toward Toledo. The village remained behind us, mute, alone in the dusky light of evening. And again the doors began to squeak like howling dogs. The full moon came out enormous, deep yellow, sad. It reminded me of the golden masks of the dead kings of Mycenae. The girls were running along behind the trucks, gasping for breath. But soon they were exhausted. They stood then on the tall threshing mills and waved their arms.

"*Arriba España! Arriba España!*" the soldiers called back to them.

But the girls only made a gesture of embrace and said nothing.

◾ THE REAL TOLEDO

◾ NIGHT HAD FALLEN when we reached the first sentry gate of Toledo. The tiny, winding streets echoed noisily. A voice was heard calling: "Zocodover Square!" The truck stopped. I jumped down hastily and cast a lightning glance around me. I seemed to be dreaming. The porticos and columns that had once enclosed the Square were gone. The stores and hotels and large pastry shops and bars had all vanished. Only one arched gate was left and over it, dangling terrifyingly in the moonlight, fragments of walls in fantastic shapes. All these splendid old buildings seemed to have turned into a theatrical set that had been knocked down as soon as the performance was over.

I had to scramble over piles of ruins, stumble over pieces of iron, broken furniture, pieces of bombs. Once this had been a street lined with stores and houses. And here, there had been a large marble staircase climbing up to the Alcázar. "When I climb this staircase," Charles V had remarked, "I feel I am really Emperor!" Where is this staircase now? The Square and the Alcázar have become one. The Alcázar has sunk, and the Square, heaped with ruins, is higher. So now they are on the same level. A high wall dangling in mid-air, broken, blackened by the flames, rose over me like a sword: the Alcázar. Nothing else survives of the famous fortress. The whole city all around it, as far as the Cathedral, is in ruins. In the moonlight, the ruins of the houses rise ethereal, full of despair, as though lamenting. By this misty light of the moon, I could make out balconies swaying back and forth, iron beams hanging loosely, skeletons of houses with broken ribs and unhinged shutters, everything deserted.

Toledo had become a canvas of El Greco, full of fiery palpitating forms, full of huge, high walls bereft of any hope. It had become a logical absurdity. The architectural layout of the city consisted now of a deceitful interplay of fleeting shadows. This vision was so magical that I hadn't the heart to leave. There must surely be some impulse toward disaster buried in the inner recesses of human beings. For they can enjoy with savage delight the spectacle of a sacked city. Toledo had grown fierce, as suits it. It had finally found a body corresponding to its own belligerent intrepid soul.

"How weary I am!" These words of El Greco, among the few left us, are marvellously attuned to the image of Toledo I had before me this night. I too was weary of all the positive logical patterns, the balanced forms, the serene life: the shops, houses, churches, wine shops. In the same way, the volcanic force of El Greco's autonomous impassioned mind must have shaken Toledo, and a host of angels must have burst like lightning over it. Nowadays, instead of angels, there are airplanes. But the mystic purpose is the same. And what is this purpose? That Toledo be stirred, delivered from its self-assured prudence and mediocrity; that it be turned to ashes and become a lofty, ghostly, pale vision—a martyr wounded on behalf of an Idea; and then that the Idea consume the body, so that the body is no longer there to obscure the flame. The essence of Toledo has remained. Only the superfluous parts have been turned to ashes.

I am ashamed to write it, but I felt no grief. Far from it! A fierce joy possessed me. The present Toledo offers more to men than the other Toledo I had known—the one that had so disappointed me when I first saw it. Then I had been expecting to find a barren rock where no water flowed, where no green plants grew, full of slender taciturn people. Instead, I had found a jolly provincial city, full of merchants, photographers, priests. Today all these people are still here: their seed cannot disappear so easily from the face of the earth. But in their eyes flash reflections from the ruins and awful scenes they have seen, as well as all the terrors they have lived through. And all this makes them less like merchants, photographers and priests.

Some rabbi once said: "God revealed His will through letters and words. But He has not yet revealed the exalted meaning between the words, in the empty spaces of the text." Here in Toledo, the words have disappeared. The text has crumbled to bits. And now for the second time (the first revelation we see in El Greco's work) these gaps in between the ruins have revealed the exalted meaning of Toledo. Not only of Toledo: of man himself, unyielding and despairing.

▪ THE SIEGE OF
THE ALCÁZAR

▪ ALL NIGHT LONG I hadn't been able to sleep. At daybreak, I began stumbling and scrambling over the mounds. The visitors to the shrine had traced a narrow footpath in among the ruins. I followed it to climb up to the Alcázar. The other men and women were wide awake now. They had come from faraway cities, and now joined the procession with me, on their way up to make this holy pilgrimage. A pale thin soldier, one of the "Free Besieged," was walking on ahead of us and telling us about it, spinning out the legend.

"Here's where the mine was. Here's where we fought. This is where we buried our dead. Here was the well where we got our water."

I strained my ears to catch every word. I was eager to learn how the spirit elaborates the crude elements of everyday life —hunger, fear, filth—transforming them into legend.

"From the early morning on, we each set about our own work. We changed watch duty. Some of us cooked. Others made bulwarks. Others used bits of broken bombs to grind the wheat in a mortar. Others carried water or slaughtered the horses or fought. There was plenty of work. The days went by."

We had entered a long passageway paved with stone slabs.

"Over there is where the women slept—over next to the horses. They suffered with us. We told them to leave, but they didn't want to. Well, what could we do? They were women. So we let them stay."

We strode over broken tables, charred books, iron beds all twisted out of shape. We went down a few steps.

"Hold your noses!" the soldier hollered to us.

There was an unbearable, disgusting stench.

"At first, we buried them outside. But when the siege began to close in on us further and further, we had to bury them in here. We didn't have much earth, so we had to bury them shallow. . . . And then the stink began . . ." The pale soldier groaned as he talked about it. "Then, on top of everything else, the water went rotten. We all got diarrhea."

He tried to laugh, but couldn't.

"What's your name?" I asked him.

By now, we'd emerged in the courtyard. Out in the fresh air again. The other pilgrims had scattered. We were alone now.

"Miguel Gómez Cascajares," was his answer. "I'm from Burgos."

On a wall in the courtyard, a bronze plaque had survived. It depicted a soldier falling into the open arms of a plump hermaphrodite figure with high pointed breasts. Over it was written in gold capital letters, all of which were still legible: "He who dies for his country is taken into the bosom of Immortality." As Miguel read it, he shook his head.

"What're you thinking of?" I asked him.

"Nothing," he answered.

We went down, climbing through the barricaded streets in silence. We had to climb over mounds of charred wood and ashes and rags. Here and there, the following words were still legible on the charred beams: "Insured Against Fire" or "Posting of Signs is Prohibited." How comic this anxious concern of the landlords, who had taken precautions for everything except the most terrifying of all: the unforesee-able. In one of the ruined mansions "Beggars Forbidden to Enter!" was still legible over the unhinged gate. But fire, can-non shots, war and death are not beggars, and they have entered.

We had reached the public square. There was a parade of schoolchildren, ten to twelve years old. They were fully equipped with guns and cartridge cases. A little boy, not more than seven years old, marched in front of them, holding a little flag. Following behind him at a brisk pace came the drummers and trumpet players and little soldiers. All their childish faces were twisted in anger, grim and unsmiling. Many of the children were biting their lips. Their eyes blazed with premature passion. Their fathers and mothers all stood in a row along the sidewalks, applauding and admiring them. We have entered on a grave, merciless era. A Chinese proverb says: "When children no longer want to play, the world's in a sad way!"

"Spain has gone mad! Spain has gone mad!" This phrase of Unamuno's was burning on my lips. I grabbed Miguel's arm. We went into a café called the Alcázar and drank a big cup of coffee. It warmed us; warmed us and we became friends.

"Even this is gone!" Miguel muttered, and his faded blue eyes grew dim. He seemed to be seeing from far far off, in a kind of haze, like a myth, this horrible adventure so steeped in filth and glory.

"I kept a diary," he said softly after a little while. He seemed to be ashamed of it. He put his hand into his shirt and pulled out some yellowed papers written in pencil.

"Here it is!" He was blushing.

I took the papers in my hands. I felt deeply touched. They were wrinkled, black, dirty with sweat stains and some dark red smudges that looked like dried blood. I began to read them. Some of the words had faded and we both bent over the paper trying to guess what they were. He filled in wherever he remembered, and so we proceeded on into the heroic simple text:

> JULY 22ND: *We have come inside and closed the gates. Colonel Moscardo has given us our orders: "My lads, take courage! The honor of Spain lies in our hands. We must not surrender! Our own people will come and free us. Behave like brave lads. Long live Spain!" We counted our numbers: 1100 men, 520 women, 50 children, 97 horses, 27 mules. My wife arrived too late to come with us. It's better that way. We've made records of what we have and what we don't have: guns, cannon, war provisions, food, water. We've put everything in order. We've arranged where the women will sleep, and where the men and horses and mules will sleep. The commandant has decreed a state of martial law. A state of siege. We've taken our posts.*

Miguel was reading quickly, in gulps, running short of breath. His yellowish finger trembled as he touched each word shakily. He turned the page:

> JULY 24TH: *We broke into several shops and took all the food we could find: rice, macaroni, beans, oil, olives, coffee, sugar. . . . Thank God! We don't have to be afraid of starving! How many days will the siege last? Ten? Fifteen? Our own people will come to free us. The cannon have begun fir-*

ing. The Reds have made their fortifications in the houses opposite us. They've seized the public square. Now the carnival's beginning! The commandant has split us into separate divisions. The "Simplon division" is supposed to dig an underground tunnel and blow up the mines the Reds are building to destroy us. The "suicide division" is going to make forays and take charge of opening up a road. I've been enrolled in this division. I'm sorry for my wife and child. But what can I do? . . . God help us!

"You were a bit afraid!" I laughed with my friend Miguel. "You were afraid, but you didn't express it in writing."

"Of course I was afraid." Miguel was talking nervously. "I'm a human being. I was afraid. But I was ashamed to say so. Not just me. I'm nobody. But do you think even the greatest heroes aren't afraid? They're shivering in their boots, I tell you, but they're ashamed of it. They're ashamed. That's the whole secret."

JULY 27TH: *Today they killed Colonel Moscardo's son.*

Miguel raised his eyes and looked at me.
"Do you have a child?" he asked me.
"No."
"Ah, well, then how could you understand?"
"Tell me, and maybe I'll be able to understand."
Miguel shook his head:
"Well then, listen. Moscardo had a child, his only son, and the Reds were holding him hostage in Madrid. Every once

in a while, *Dring-a-dring!* The telephone. 'Surrender the Alcázar, or we'll kill your son.'

" 'I will not surrender!' Moscardo would answer back, hanging up the telephone.

"One day the child himself phoned him. 'Father, they're telling me here if you don't surrender the Alcázar, they're going to kill me. Don't surrender, Papa! What's my life worth to me? Nothing!'

"And Moscardo gave him this answer: 'Don't worry, my dear child. I won't surrender. Your life is very precious. But Spain's honor is even more precious. Long live Spain, child!'

"After a few days, the Reds telephoned Moscardo again: 'Surrender the Alcázar now; otherwise we're going to kill your son!'

" 'I will not surrender!'

" 'Then don't hang up the telephone. You are going to hear us shoot your son.'

"Moscardo did not hang up the telephone. And he heard the shot. The Reds had killed his child. . . ."

Miguel had cast his eyes down. They were full of tears, and he was ashamed. His voice emerged hoarse and stifled:

"Damn these quarrels that split men apart!" he exclaimed. "Damn war! Damnation on it!"

He seemed very upset as he turned the pages. Then he read further:

> JULY 29TH: *We are eating well. We kill four horses every day, and we've gotten used to the booming of the cannon. But we have one great grief: we don't know what's become of our people. Where can they be? When will they turn up? They said they'd take Madrid in four days. The four days are over now. Why haven't they taken it?*

"This was our greatest torture," Miguel went on. "They'd cut off all our lines of communication, and left only one telephone with the Red commandant of Toledo, that scoundrel Major Bardelo. Every day he kept telephoning, telling us, 'Surrender! Surrender!' And he tried to break us by telling a heap of lies intended to terrify us, such as: 'Our men have scattered early on!' or 'Franco has been killed and the revolution washed away in blood!'

"But Moscardo always shouted back: 'I'm not going to surrender!' and hung up.

"The Reds were furious. They brought an army from Madrid, tanks and airplanes. Iron shells began to fall like rain. They fortified themselves inside all the houses near us. They piled sacks of dirt high in the windows, on the balconies and rooftops, and began firing on us. They had a loudspeaker, and blared over it: 'We'll pluck out your eyes! We'll roast you over the fire! We'll disgrace your women, if you won't surrender!' But we kept quiet. 'Patience,' we used to tell ourselves. 'Patience! Today or tomorrow our men will appear. . . .'

"But the days were going by, and nobody appeared. So some of our men got scared. One day, in a raid by the 'suicide division' for provisions, ten of our comrades ran away and went over to the Reds. I have their names written here. But what good are they? Let's turn the page. They're a disgrace to us. . . ."

He turned the page and began to read as follows:

AUGUST 5TH: *We're retreating further and further inside. We've let go of the buildings outside the ramparts. We're all of us squeezed inside the fortress. We've sent the women and children down to the cellars. It's damp down there and dark, and the holes are full of rats. But it's safe. Our electricity's been cut off. We're burning fat from the horses and mules to make candles, so we have a little light. Thank God, the library was full of big thick books bound in leather, so we could barricade the windows. Everything's running smoothly. And yesterday, we had a great success! Our commandant summoned the "suicide division."*

"Lads," he said to us, "a man must always imagine the worst possible and always be prepared. Well, this siege may drag on many more days still. So let's take our measures. I've heard there's a warehouse full of wheat nearby. So, to action! Make the sign of the cross, and try to get out tonight. I'll give you a man to guide you. And carry away as much wheat as you can, lads!"

We set out at midnight, very softly so that the Reds wouldn't get wind of us. We found the warehouse and crawled into it through a hole made by the cannon. The warehouse was stuffed with big bags of wheat. We took them on our shoulders and went on transporting them till daybreak. And there are still some left. We'll empty it all. There are times when not only a man's life but his honor, too, depend on a dry crust of bread. We have plenty of wheat. Our honor is safe. Long live Spain!

"You see," Miguel went on, "we also had our joys. Don't believe the newspaper accounts; they say we were gloomy all day long and all night long and the sound of laughter was never heard, and our women never laid off lamenting. We had that too, of course. We were only human. We saw violence all around us. We saw our comrades being killed. But we also had our joys. We used to tell jokes to pass the time. We felt very gay the times when our food was cooking and when we ate it, and later, when we lit our cigarettes and started smoking. At first we had quite a lot of tobacco, but curses on it! It got used up. Finally one day, we didn't even have a pinch of snuff left. It drove us mad. And can you believe it? One night we made a foray to break into a tobacco shop and raid it. We were risking our lives and limbs for a cigarette. Well, there's a human being for you. . . ."

He turned two or three pages:

"Here, I'm writing to my wife," he said. "Just to blow off a bit of steam. What could we do? A woman's like tobacco. A whim; you get used to her. And then when you can't have her, your head whirs. Your brain goes foggy. So you sit down and write to her, and that way, you blow off a bit of steam."

On the next page, Miguel had scrawled a date in big letters: AUGUST 15TH. The hand that had written it had obviously been trembling. With joy or grief? And down below, in red pencil, he'd sketched a sun with huge rays. At the tip of each ray, he'd written the name of a city: Madrid, Seville, Burgos, Barcelona. And over the furthest ray, at the tip, in capital letters, the word Berlin.

"What's this sketch?" I asked him.

"Ah!" cried Miguel, and his eyes flashed. "This was a great joy; I think our greatest joy of all. Greater, God forgive me, than smoking or women. Listen, and you'll see why. This sun you see painted here is our radio. That day I felt so happy I couldn't write. So, instead, I drew. I told you how they'd cut off all our communication with the outside world. We had neither telegraph equipment nor a radio. So we were isolated from the whole world. We had no idea what was happening to our own side. We felt suffocated. That was the most awful part of the siege. We were suffocated. Then sud-

denly, one day, the 15th of August, our two mechanics found
a few electric batteries in the physics laboratory of the school.
And they succeeded in making the radio work! All at once,
we were back in touch with the whole world. It seemed as
though the siege were over. '*Arriba España!*' But you can
imagine how upset we were when we could only get the
Madrid station. And what didn't they say! Lies! Lies! That
the rebels had wiped out thousands of innocent people. That
they'd allowed the Moroccans to plunder and pillage and
burn whole villages. They were even saying that the Alcázar
had surrendered. They were actually describing the surrender
in full detail—what time we surrendered, how the besieged
came out in groups of five, without their weapons. Some of
us burst out laughing when we heard these lies. Others
cursed. 'Shut up, you silly imbeciles!' someone shouted. 'Let
them say whatever they please. We're here, and we're not going to surrender! So take heart! Today is a great feast day—
the Virgin's name day. Let's celebrate it.' So we took our
places for the dance and struck up the tune. Some of us remembered the hymns to the Virgin and started chanting
them. Two or three days went by. Our mechanics kept on
working. Then one evening, when the cannon fire had
stopped, we got the station in Milan. We got the station in
Lisbon. These were our friends! Our friends! Then we
learned everything. We understood what had happened. We
had taken Seville. Franco was coming up from the south.
General Mola was coming down from the north. They were
advancing victoriously. They'd taken Badajoz. The two
armies had met, and shortly they would be closing the in-
famous city of Madrid in their iron grip. '*Arriba España!*'
echoed through the underground passages of the Alcázar. '*Arriba* Cristo el Rey!' And we all embraced and wept with joy.
The women heard and came running from the kitchens and

the laundry rooms. And then we started a rousing festive dance. All of us began singing the Hymn of the Alcázar. . . ."

"You'd written a hymn too?"

"Of course we had! One of our comrades wrote the words, Alfredo Martínez Leal. And Martin Hill set it to music."

"And do you remember it?"

"If they cut me in a thousand pieces, each small piece of me would still be able to sing it."

Little by little, as he went on talking, my friend Miguel had grown feverishly excited. He was reliving all those heroic days. He was animated, flushed. His faded blue eyes flashed now. And right there in the middle of the café he began singing, in a low voice, the Hymn of the Alcázar:

> *Children of Spain,*
> *Fight bravely and*
> *Save our native land.*
> *Traitors and malefactors,*
> *All ye who spurn Religion,*
> *Your bullets and bombs*
> *Will never knock down*
> *The Alcázar to the ground.*

Insignificant words, but all the same, Miguel's eyes had filled with tears. He was laughing and crying at once. His past joys and griefs were awake now inside him, and he felt stifled by them. He must have longed to scream or smash a glass or break the mirrors. But he was ashamed, and, instead, he broke down in quiet sobs.

"And we had other joys, too! Other joys!" he added suddenly. "On the 22nd of August—look here, I've written it down. We raised our eyes to the sky, and what did we see?

Like an angel, it seemed to us. One of our side's airplanes zoomed over us like lightning. It threw us an envelope and got away before the Reds could fire at it! General Franco had sent a letter to our commandant, Colonel Moscardo. What it said, we don't know. But that day, Moscardo smiled for the first time since his son's murder. 'My lads,' he said to us, 'God is with us! God is with Spain! Courage!' We took courage. We began printing a newspaper on the stencil machine. We called it the *Alcázar*. You see, the radio we had was very soft. How could everyone hear it! So we printed all the news in our little newspaper. Of course not every day . . . because now the Reds had started bombarding us with heavy fire, night and day, so that we couldn't hear anything on the radio. But whenever we did hear any news, we printed it in our newspaper, on the stencil machine. We printed diagrams and maps of where our army was and how it was advancing. The last page of the newspaper was the amusement section: riddles, puns, games, jokes to pass our time."

Miguel ordered another coffee. He took out his tobacco pouch and cigarette paper, rolled a cigarette and began smoking. He looked at me with his blue eyes so full of fire now.

"But don't get the idea our life was easy!" he said to me suddenly. "Now that it's all over, I don't know why, but I feel ashamed to say how much we suffered. I prefer to talk about the good things. Just the same, read here!"

He bent over and showed me a page, pointing to it with his finger. I read:

AUGUST 27TH: *One of our wells was broken by the bombs. The water spilled. We've made it into a burial place. Today I buried my friend Aurelio Mendoza. He'd been on lookout duty up in the tower, when a mortar shell fell. My friend and two*

*other comrades were blown to bits. I collected his
remains with a shovel and wheelbarrow. We raised
the slabs in the bottom of the well and buried the
dead there and covered them with earth. They've
already begun to rot and smell. . . . Yesterday a
woman fainted.*

Miguel shook his head.

"I told you how we didn't have enough earth to bury
them deep. Then later, there were lots of them, too. By now,
the Reds had brought in huge cannon and were firing on us
continuously. They were determined to trample down the
Alcázar. They threw thousands of bombs at us. I don't know
how many. But thousands! And what did we have for am-
munition? One tiny cannon, which we'd rigged up in the
library. This is all we had to fight with. Then, when the bom-
bardment stopped and they charged us, we used to fall on
them with ordinary rifles and a few machine guns. I told you
that when there was a dark night we used to go out secretly
and grab wheat and tobacco and anything we could find. But
the Reds caught on to us, and what did the bastards do?
They turned strong searchlights on us, which cast a blind-
ing light on the Alcázar. So the Alcázar glared in floodlights
all night long. How could we show our faces now! Well, there
were some good points too. We didn't have any fat left from
the horses and mules, and our candles had all gone out. So
after all, these spotlights gave us our only light at night. By
this light, our women ground the wheat in large mortars.
They had to use bits of broken bombs to grind it till a skillful
mechanic there with us contrived an electric mill out of a
small automobile motor. Then our poor women had a slightly
easier time of it."

"What did the women do during the siege?"

"What did they do? You don't think they rested a single moment, the poor things? They were cooking and kneading the dough and baking. They washed the dishes and clothes. They swept and patched our clothes and served as nurses. They suffered just as much as the men. That's how Spanish women are, believe me! There're some who say they're only good for sex and songs and frivolity, castanet players! But the devil take anyone who says so! The Spanish women are indomitable mothers and serious faithful companions to their husbands. They sit and guard their doorways like dogs!"

Miguel sighed, looking far off again. Evening had begun to fall. A silvery murky light flooded the ruins. The great arched marble gate, the Puerta de la Sangre, the only one still standing, shone lonely, sad, utterly empty.

"Ah, Miguel, my friend, read on," I said.

My friend turned back in my direction again, and began thumbing through his pages.

"Ah, well, from here on, it's all the same," he said. "Bombs and more bombs! By now, they'd hemmed us in on all sides. Every hour, every second, some new part of the Alcázar was crumbling. Every second the Reds were expecting us to surrender. They'd surrounded us like mad dogs. Azaña had come to watch us die. Largo Caballero had come . . . Margarita Nelken and la Pasionara! We were holding on to our lives by the skin of our teeth. 'Hold on bravely!' we were shouting to each other. 'Hold on bravely! Our side will be coming to free us!'

"Look here:

AUGUST 29TH: *Our radio brought us big news today: General Yanguas' regiment is advancing on Toledo. The Reds have been decisively beaten. In the last battle, 200 Reds were killed and 1,000 wounded. Five cannon were captured by us, three machine guns and one tank. Yanguas is advancing with overwhelming strength. Soon Toledo will be ours!*

"We wept with joy, shouting like madmen: 'Long live Spain! Long live Christ!' We couldn't sleep all night because of our joy. In the morning, we looked out toward the west, and out toward the south. We were expecting Yanguas to appear with his army. But nothing! Nothing . . . that day . . . or the next day. Or the next. After our great hope, our hearts began to feel exhausted. We'd grown terribly thin from bad living conditions, lack of sleep, all the terrors. And we were sick from the rotten water. Our poor souls couldn't wait calmly any longer."

A Guardia Civil came into the café.

"Hello there, Miguel!" he called. "*Qué tal?* How're you?"

But my friend had sunk into a kind of impenetrable horror and didn't even hear him.

"From that day on," he continued softly, "our suffering began to be unbearable. Three of our comrades went mad. Many of us suffered nervous breakdowns and started shrieking. Others would suddenly burst into forced laughter for no reason at all. A man's poor nerves, you see, aren't strong as rope. They can't hold out forever. Day and night now, we could hear the gritch-gritch, gritch-gritch—Death boring through the granite underneath us, coming ever closer. Do you understand? Miners had come from Asturia and had begun digging through the rock. They were going to drill a mine underneath the Alcázar. Day and night, we could hear their machines drilling away with that scratching sound against the rock. They were making a tunnel. They were getting closer and closer. When they finally reached a point right under our feet, they would pile up the dynamite and ignite it. Then we'd all be blasted high in the air, fortress and all of us along with it! We felt as though our final hour were approaching . . .

". . . 13th, 14th, 15th, 16th, 17th of September. See what I've written here. For all these dates, just one word: *Terror! Terror! Terror! Terror!* We were all—don't pay any attention to what the newspapers say now!—all of us trembling with fear. By now the miners were under our very feet. They must have piled up the dynamite by now. Moment to moment, we were expecting them to ignite the spark and blow us all to smithereens. Anyone who was not in the Alcázar can go around now exclaiming, 'Heroes! Heroes! Not for a single instant did their hearts tremble!' Hah! The devil take them! Lies, lies! Listen to me. For whole days and nights we were trembling like rabbits in our hearts. We were human, I tell you, not stones. And we were trembling. But you may ask me why didn't we surrender then? Ah, our honor wouldn't let us; would not let us!

"During the night of the 17th/18th September, bugles were heard in Toledo. The loudspeaker began blaring. "The whole population of Toledo must leave at once! Must get outside the city walls! Danger of death!" The inhabitants began running toward the plain. They took refuge in the hill opposite. It was cold that night. A strong wind was blowing. And everyone . . . women and men alike were rushing as far from Toledo as they could. They all knew that in a few hours it was going to explode in mid-air. At midnight the Reds telephoned Colonel Moscardo: 'The mine is finished. We've piled up seven tons of explosives. We have only to press a button, and you'll be blown sky-high. Surrender!'

"No answer. Colonel Moscardo put down the telephone receiver. All of us stood there, pale, our hair on end. We could hear the machines still drilling away beneath us. And we waited. Nobody said anything. Nobody wept. All of us still, silent, yellow as the dead, just stood and waited.

"At 7:00 A.M. on the 18th of September, a workman pressed the button. The fuse was ignited! A terrible earthquake of a sound. The earth gaped open. All Toledo was shaken. A column of fire and smoke shot up in the sky. Huge fragments of the fortress avalanched down as far as the city. The big southwest tower was scattered in tiny pieces. The whole Alcázar was suffocated in smoke. A quarter of an hour passed, half an hour. An hour passed. What had become of the besieged? There was no sight of anyone behind the smoke. The Reds, with their bayonets cocked and their hand grenades ready, finally made up their minds to rush on the fortress. They were sure we'd all been buried under the ruins. As yet, no one had emerged from underground.

"The Reds leaped over the gaping ditches and strode over the huge boulders, till they reached the big courtyard devastated by the bombs. They stopped short, as though suddenly some mysterious fear had come over them. They looked toward the underground passages with glazed eyes, and came no closer.

" 'Up and at them, comrades!' someone shouted, laughing. 'Now the ghosts are going to show!' He'd no sooner finished his words than a hand grenade exploded, and then another, and another, and another, showering the Reds. The ghosts had sprung out of the ground.

" 'Long live Spain!' we cried. 'Long live Christ!' We tangled in man-to-man combat. We'd gone wild: overjoyed at being safe and sound, mad to slaughter the bastards. We were like madmen. The Reds couldn't hold out against us. They began tumbling down from the fortress. They'd tacked their tattered Red flag up over our tower. We tore it down.

All of us—men, women, children—foaming at the mouth, roaring 'Spain! Spain! Spain!'

"We set watch-duty, then went down into the underground passages. We started dancing and singing. We were mad, I tell you. Whatever we did, we owe to our madness and not our common sense. Our common sense whispered to us night and day: 'Surrender!' Our madness bellowed: 'Don't surrender!' And we listened to our madness. And so everything that happened happened. We embraced each other down there in the underground passages, and touched each other. We couldn't yet believe we were alive. . . . Have you ever felt such a joy?"

"Never!" I answered.

"May God never wish it on you!" Miguel said, with a bitter smile.

He stopped talking, and I realized that he was trembling.

"You're cold, Miguel?"

"Yes," he answered.

"Bring us a cognac here!"

They brought him the cognac. He drank it down in one gulp, warmed up, took heart, went on:

"During those days, the priest Camarasas arrived from Madrid. The Reds had sent him. He performed the church liturgy, holding the cross in his hands and crying out: 'Surrender! God's curse on any man who stands against the Law!' He turned toward the panic-stricken women: 'You'll all go to Hell,' he shouted at them, 'if you don't surrender! Pity your souls!' The women wept. Two newly-born children were baptized by him. Two old men who had died were buried, and he chanted the death liturgy over their graves. We all took Holy Communion. And then we drove him off. 'You'll go to Hell!' the damnable priest cried out as he left. 'You'll go to Hell!'

" 'Arriba España!' we cried back to him, from up there.

"From that day on, the Reds were ferocious. 'Burn them alive! Pour gasoline on the walls and set them on fire! The Alcázar must fall at once!' They kept telephoning the Red commandant of Toledo from Madrid. The Red general, Assensio, who would be coming from Madrid, gave the orders. The fire department loaded its trucks with gasoline and lined them up in rows in Zocodover Square.

"On the 19th of September, when we leaned from the fortress early in the morning, we could see the fire engines speeding toward us, with their hoses ready to spray the gasoline in sheets. 'They're going to burn us alive, the devils!' we whispered in terror. And the gasoline actually began pouring all over the fortress. We were lost. And then will you believe it? . . . But we were mad. We did unbelievable things. A young man leaped from a window. He couldn't have been more than twenty. He had only a revolver in his hand. He rushed out, grabbed the hoses, and turned them toward Santa Cruz, where the Reds had their fortifications. Then the lad fell, riddled with bullet holes.

"Our hearts were fired. We rushed down. Once again we fought them man to man. We were no longer mere men. We'd turned into demons. Sitting here now calmly in the café, I can't believe it . . . Was it really me, Miguel Cascajares of Burgos, who did all these brave deeds? But I was never the brave sort. I was a placid little teacher with a bad lung condition. I used to cough, catch cold, sweat heavily at the slightest provocation. I was used to good food and my own medicines. How did I ever manage to live through the Alcázar? Mysterious, mysterious! And what's more: from that time on, I haven't coughed any more or spit—after all those hardships and terrors, I'm cured, by God!

"But enough of Miguel!" he said laughing. "Back to the

Alcázar! The next day, the 20th of September, the cannon
and gunfire started up again. The Reds, we have to hand it
to them, fought like men too. They attacked with hand
grenades and metal containers of gasoline. They lit fires all
around us. But we put them out as soon as they were lit.
They nailed their bloodstained flag over our ramparts. We
tore it down. And they nailed it back up! How fierce they
were, the bastards! Twenty or thirty stubborn men advancing
into the very heart of the Alcázar, preferring to be killed
rather than leave. And then more of them would come. They
got as far as our kitchens, poured the gasoline there and
ignited it. All night long the Alcázar blazed. The next day,
three airplanes flew over us. Our side! They threw us food
and a letter: 'Courage, lads! General Varela will soon be
there. Hold on! Be brave!'

"Of the four towers of the Alcázar, only one was still
standing. Today that one fell too. Everything around us was
collapsing. We huddled in the underground passages. For
some days now, we'd begun feeling the hunger. We were no
longer killing four horses a day: just one for the 1800 human
beings still left. Each day we each got one piece of bread
that was like mud and half a liter of dirty water. And the
horrible smell, my God! We stank, both the living and the
dead! We looked at each other in disgust. How could we
hold out? I tell you, it's a mysterious thing! And as if that
wasn't enough! The machines had started up again under
our very feet, digging through the rock, gritch-gritch! They
were building a new mine against us. 'Don't be afraid!'
Colonel Moscardo kept saying to us. 'Don't be afraid! God
is with us!' . . . But we were afraid. 'My God,' I used to
say very often, 'just let them kill me and get it over with!
I can't stand it any more!'

"On the 25th of September, the earth shook again. They'd

set off the new mines. All the walls that were still upright collapsed. You know where the church of San Domingo is? Well, one of the trucks was hurled all the way from here to the courtyard there. The pit that explosion made was 100 meters in diameter and 70 meters deep. The tanks rushed in at once to occupy the fortress. They'd reached us now. They were in the Alcázar, and then suddenly, the ghosts sprang out of the earth again. It was us, still full of life! 'They're still alive!' the Reds cried out in terror. We tangled with them again and bowled them over again. We set the watch duties and waited, kneeling there, with rifles.

"All that day, silence. Not even a cannon shot, or a rifle shot. What was going on? Another sort of terror overwhelmed us now. 'They're contriving something new for us, the bastards!' we thought to ourselves, but said nothing. We waited. During the night, an awful thunderstorm broke out. Covered by the darkness and the rain, ten of us went down into the city to find something to eat—a tin of sardines or some cigarettes. We raided two stores, loaded up and came back. Not a single Red. The streets were empty, the houses bolted, pitch dark! 'Something's up, lads!' we said to our comrades. 'We must none of us fall asleep.'

"But the next day, around dawn, we saw that the mouths of the big cannon over on the hill of Aliquares were no longer pointed at us. They had been turned toward the west. 'Our men are on their way!' an officer cried. 'Look! They've turned their cannon westward. Our men are coming, lads!'

"On the 26th of September, around twilight, as we stood there rigid and silent, our eyes glued to the west, we saw our army advancing. Our national flag, our brothers! Deliverance! We made signals and they signaled back to us. Of course we must have been overjoyed, but we no longer had the strength to feel joy. Our army entered Toledo. General Varela himself was leading it. The Reds had gone. Only the most fanatic stayed behind, lying in wait behind their doors and windows. They had raised embankments in the streets. On the 27th of September began the war from house to house, and street to street. Thousands of Reds were killed that day. The rest of them escaped hastily, in the direction of Madrid. At 9:00 P.M. our national army scaled the Alcázar. Leaping over the ruins, climbing over the broken towers, they reached the main courtyard. And then we came up from underground. . . . Everyone who saw us there describes how they'd never seen anything like it in their lives. Nor will they ever. It seems we were no longer human. We were ghosts. We'd become skeletons. Our skin was all wrinkled and yellowish, flapping loosely over our bones. Our eyes were enormous and glazed. We were unshaven, filthy, ragged. Our knees trembled. We couldn't shout or jump up and down, we were so exhausted. Until that moment, we'd held out bravely—so long as we were in the grip of danger. But all of a sudden, the moment salvation came, we were paralyzed. . . . We could no longer stand up straight.

"We came up from underground: policemen, soldiers, volunteers, students of the Gymnastic School, workmen, children, women, the five mules left over and one horse— the last one—all the besieged of the Alcázar. In the main courtyard, Colonel Moscardo went up to General Varela, saluted him and said: 'My General, all in order here!' "

■ MADRID GOES TO HER
DOOM: PART I

■ THE RUINS OF the Alcázar were still warm when I reached Toledo. The cheeks of my friend, Miguel, still had the hero's pallor. The legend was still fizzling like fermenting wine. Each of the besieged I met added something from his own imagination or memory. He was creating history, molding the epic in his own image and likeness. All that was superfluous was discarded. The essential was being discovered. Little by little, the rumors crystallized and the legend assumed a definite shape. This was how I lived my first days in Toledo: eating and drinking and talking with these heroes, who have been enshrined in history for all time. When the Alcázar died, it became immortal.

And El Greco? Among all the cannon and explosives and fires and bloodshed, the great Cretan, El Greco, was lost. He comes before the weapons. He comes after them. He divines the future and immortalizes the past. But now, in the midst of this horrendous tornado of fratricide, who cares about his apostles and angels? The apostles have other names now. They are called Franco and Caballero; Molas and la Pasionara. And his angels are called airplanes. Later on, another El Greco will come (God willing!) to immortalize these present ephemeral creatures and machines swaying in the autumn air of Spain, during these blood-washed epoch-making months.

The present Toledo, perfected as it had been by the

explosions and the bombs, was so like El Greco's vision that as I wandered below its fierce and battle-scarred, unyielding walls, I seemed to be floating inside some work of El Greco. And so I felt no need of seeing the miniatures of his works squeezed into their thick gold frames.

One stormy gray twilight on a narrow little street in front of the Church of Santo Tomé, I suddenly caught sight of soldiers on their way to war, in groups of four. The electric light on the corner lit them harshly. The nozzles of their guns flashed for a moment, and their bayonets and brass buttons. They were all beardless youths, boys. Their eyes flashed strangely. Their cheeks were pale, emaciated. They raised their arms with the cry: "*Viva Cristo el Rey!* Long live Christ our King!" I stopped short. I felt a shudder pass through me. Weren't these El Greco's soldiers in the "Espolio" and the "Saint Maurice"? The people painted by the old Cretan had come to life, flooding over the streets of Toledo, raising that same ecstatic cry: "*Viva Cristo el Rey!*"

I suddenly sensed that what I had just seen was far bloodier and far more bitter than the colors of El Greco, far more in harmony with our own desperate condemned spirit of today. Each epoch has its own battlefield: religion, art, science, industry, war. The vital person is he who fights in the field chosen by his own epoch. We have entered on a military epoch, and so today, the only vital people are those who work in cooperation with it, in this most dangerous field.

Let us then perform our present-day duty insofar as we are able. The cannon shots from Toledo sound further and further away. Every day the nationalistic army is advancing on Madrid—8, 10, 15 kilometers. Will it seize possession of her, or will it not?

The road between Toledo and Madrid is broad, paved

with tar, about 70 kilometers long. Early in the morning we'd passed the Arab sentry posts and come down to the plain. My heart is heavy. I am on my way to watch Madrid going to her doom.

Cars full of officers, truckloads of young soldiers singing away and frantically howling Moroccans. A brilliant sun, bright blue sky. Two or three old men tilling the fields. Old women on their doorsteps waving the fascist salute, awkwardly and in mortal terror. Ruined fields, walls riddled with holes, doors, houses, shops gaping open, lentils, beans, sugar scattered over the sidewalks. Here and there along the curbs of the roads or in the fields, the earth swollen and billowing with graves.

The further one goes, the more one is aware that the terrible vagabond of war has passed here. Water canteens thrown on the ground, army boots, workmen's shirts, blood. Clouds of flies and crows. Horses with gangrened drumlike bellies lying on their backs in the fields, their legs sticking up in the air. The dogs and horses and mules are also fighting and being killed. Some of them go with the Reds, some with the Blacks. They rush out on top of each other, howling and not knowing why. Yesterday I'd seen a peasant in Toledo dragging a miserable black dog by the rope. It was yelping with pain.

"*Hombre!*" I called to the peasant. "What's wrong with your dog? He's in pain!" The peasant had just laughed. Without answering, he'd stretched his hand and showed me a deep wound on the dog's forehead. When I bent down, what did I see? A cross branded there with a burning iron. Blood was still pouring from it. The fanatic peasant had forced even his dog to turn martyr for the Catholic religion!

Getafe. The village is still warm, still smoking from the

bloody and violent tangle. On the walls: painted hammers and sickles. Tattered Red flags on the balconies. A smell of explosives in the air. In the middle of the square, a corpse flat on its back, its face frozen; its glassy eyes stare at the sky, fixed and terror-stricken. As I bend over, I see an envelope sticking out of his pocket: it's a letter. I draw it out of the pocket and take it with trembling hand.

In the coffee houses, the mirrors are broken. As though in panic, the chairs are all piled up to the ceiling. The grocery stores have all been raided and left wide open. Everything has disappeared from them. Only a sign high up on the wall: "*Vendemos solo al contado!* We sell only for cash!" In a notary public's office, the contracts have turned to shreds and wings and flown out the window, scattering the land-lords' interests all over the road. In the tiny village square, there's a soldier sitting all alone in front of a bombed-out wine shop. He has a phonograph on top of a little iron table. He's playing records on it. And down at his feet lies a long narrow cask of wine. Every so often, the soldier stoops down, opens the cork and takes a swig. Then he leans his two elbows back on the table again, listens to his record, groans, and takes another drink. He seems very upset.

"What's the matter with him?" I ask a soldier.

"Ah, he's in a bad mood! This used to be his wine shop. And they killed his wife too. . . ."

I climbed a height to look out. Beyond, wrapped in the faintest of mists, Madrid lay spread out—serene, smiling, vo-luptuous. With field glasses, I could see the palace clearly, and her gardens and streets and squares. A huge Red flag waved over the skyscraper post office. There were clusters of autumnal clouds passing swiftly over the beloved city. One moment they covered her lightly with their shadow and

Madrid was dark. The next moment they vanished and Madrid sparkled again, as though she were laughing. It seemed as though some sad thought was passing through her mind: one moment, she forgot it, and the next, it was back again.

"Aren't you sorry for her?" I asked an officer who was near me.

"For whom?"

"Madrid."

"She's Red . . . When she's White again . . ."

I felt afraid. For a long time I gazed at Madrid insatiably, as though I were saying goodbye to her forever. Now I was certain that the age we are living in is an abominable one and that the spirit is in danger. We would have to move quickly now, if we wanted to see whatever things of beauty are still left on the earth. Before tomorrow maybe, or the day after tomorrow for sure, when the bombs and airplanes and dark powers would come and destroy them. Eclipse. We watch clearly and in torment the black wings spreading and enshrouding the spirit in darkness.

At that instant, I heard a terrific noise: the airplanes in the sky. The soldiers were jumping up and down for joy.

"Nuestros! Nuestros!" they yelled. "Our side! Our side! Now they'll grind her to dust!"

The iron birds got bigger and bigger as they approached. At first they were like cranes, then big eagles, and then when they were rumbling over us, they looked like horrible winged monsters with a human being inside their heads instead of a brain. There were nine of them, flying in a straight line, three by three. In a few seconds, they would reach Madrid.

I held my breath. I was overpowered by awe and horror at the diabolical power of the human mind. Also by an unbearable sadness. The carnivorous shrieking birds were over the heart of Madrid. Then all at once, the sound of rhythmic dry thuds echoed cro!-cro!-cro! nine times.

"They're bombing!" the officer shouted, jumping for joy. "*Arriba España!*"

He'd hardly uttered this cry, when nine dense columns of smoke rose over the southern part of Madrid, in even lines, just like the battle formation of the airplanes. Nine holes in the viscera of Madrid. With each bomb, it seemed as though a whole neighborhood were being turned to dust and scattered in the air.

"Each bomb weighs 200 kilos!" the officer announced, as he scanned Madrid eagerly.

The clouds of smoke scattered. I strained my ear. I wanted to hear the cries of pain that must be coming from Madrid. She'd been heavily wounded and must be in pain. There had been explosions in many of her houses.

But then, from behind Madrid, we heard a heavy metallic noise. We could see seven iron hawks streaming out under the clouds. Then the nine airplanes swerved violently and rushed into combat. We caught our breath. I had stretched out flat on the ground to watch. An air battle is one of the most beautiful spectacles devised by the satanic human mind. It has a magic grace and power and a simple nobility, with all the nimbleness of a bird and the human brain combined. One feels a strange rare pride in being a man— that mysterious, inventive, restless organism, that yearning which is forever growing sharper, which is diabolically arrogant, which no longer accepts the heavy earth-bound and sea routes of our forefathers, which has shifted the combat to the lightest, most spacious element: air.

The nine fascist bombers had formed a circle: a pulsing

dance. The seven Republican fighter planes were more mobile. They rose and swooped in graceful, lightning-swift curves, zooming down head first, like hawks. They seemed to be playing—like a dance in the springtime, with the young girls in the center and the strange bridegrooms encircling them, vying for those who were strongest and most graceful. But we heard the sharp crackle of the machine guns. The dance was shattered; the lines were broken. They moved like whirlwinds in the air: a whole host of airplanes fleeing, then returning, then vanishing in a flash into the clouds. Suddenly one of the planes began to make a peculiar noise. Its right wing had come loose, and all at once, violently, like a comet, it shot down to the ground. It fell in back of a hill in Madrid and disappeared. At the same instant, we heard a cry of horror near us. A bomber had crashed. It was turning over and over with a fearful racket. About 200 meters ahead of us, it crashed into the fields.

In agony we all ran toward it. We got there, and saw the whole field strewn with bits of aluminum, broken motors and cartridges. Buried head down in the ground: a shapeless wreck, the airplane.

"*Nuestro!*" the officer muttered, biting his lips.

We could see blood all over the ground. And, among the twisted shattered remnants, we made out a slimy shape—red mincemeat, a leather helmet.

"The pilot!" cried the soldiers, as they started clearing away the pieces of iron and machinery and broken wings.

In spite of longing to get away, I forced myself to stay there: to watch; not to lose a single drop of the horror. A stretcher arrived. The soldiers bent over and handful by handful, scooped the human pulp onto the stretcher.

■　■

In dead silence I jumped into our car. We were going on: Getafe, Parla, Alcorcón, Leganés. I got out. Today the road ahead was no longer passable. There were huge cannon with their mouths turned on Madrid. The earth shook at every cannon shot. The village church had lost its roof and belfry. Its bells had fallen and sunk halfway into the ground. Once more the airplanes rumbled in the sky.

"*Rojos! Rojos!*" a voice shouted. "Scatter yourselves!"

We scattered. Some of us crouched in the fields. Others burrowed into the church. Others leaned against the wall to watch. There were only a few Moroccans who didn't budge. They'd lit fires behind the church and were cooking there. From somewhere they'd dug up some cherry velvet armchairs and were sitting in them. They'd carted a big wooden bed over and were chopping it up and throwing it into the fire. The airplanes reverberated over us a moment and passed by. Then a peasant appeared on his donkey, laden with two baskets of grapes. We filled our fists with sourish black grapes, and felt refreshed.

We moved on with my companion, the officer. Now we were approaching the front lines. The soldiers were firing away, stretched flat on the ground behind gunny sacks full of earth. We drew back and hid ourselves behind the branches of the trees. The bombs whizzed by. From time to time, a shriek could be heard. Someone had been killed. Sometimes the shriek was louder: right next to us. I turned. A Falange soldier, all doubled up and tangled in his cape, lay there writhing. A bomb must have cut off his leg, because I could see some way off a chopped-off leg with a bloodstained army boot, motionless.

In back of a row of trees, hand grenades boomed with dry thuds repeated time after time. And a noise of trees cracking.

"The Moroccans must have captured another tank," my friend said to me. "They fall on it, climb up, throw hand grenades, kill the driver and seize it."

"Isn't it dangerous for you to teach the Moroccans to kill the Spaniards?" I said.

The officer shrugged his shoulders.

"They're our best soldiers," came his answer. "Fearless, disciplined, devoted. With amazing ease, they learn how to use weapons, cannon, hand grenades. They have a very keen sense of sight and hearing. Even at night they can see. And like animals, they can hear even the faintest noise. When they make war, we ourselves feel terrified."

I didn't say anything. But one day, we will bitterly regret having taught them to fight and kill us now. We are sacrificing the future for our immediate need. One day all these strong races will fall on us. But today, no one pays any attention to this. I was pleased to see this historical law: the descent of the barbarians, advancing in this way, mercilessly, paving the way for itself. Indeed we ourselves are paving the way for it to encamp in our midst. But no one can see this till the fullness of time will make it manifest. The fullness of time will speak, but by then it will be too late.

Night had fallen. The clouds scattered. The stars looked big, autumnal, hanging over Madrid and her enemies. The cannon shots had ceased. The airplanes lay concealed in their caves. And the soldiers had lit fires to warm themselves and cook.

How could I go back to Toledo now and leave Madrid! Hungrily I watched her veiled in the smoky mists of the evening. Night rose up from the earth, black and threatening, hiding the gardens and streets and houses. A Falange soldier gave me a printed pamphlet found inside the knapsack of a Red who'd been killed:

1. Love Madrid above all else.
2. Keep your oath to die for your beloved Madrid.
3. Bless her soil with your blood.
4. Be an honor to our heroic forefathers, who fell for the Idea.
5. Die killing.
6. Refuse to surrender your wife to the Moroccans.
7. Defend your liberties with tooth and nail, up to the last moment.
8. Strike out against falsehood and slavery.
9. Drive the savage Moroccans from our land.
10. Make Madrid the tomb of Franco.

As I perused the ten commandments of the Reds, I felt someone's hot breath panting down my back. Five or six Moroccans were squatting on the ground behind me. With their guns on their knees, they were staring at Madrid. Their eyes smoldered with ineffable lust. They were seeing Paradise: a rich city, full of gold and silks and women, and slain Infidels.

I came back and lay down near the church, between those two bells half buried in the ground. I closed my eyes. A smell of earth; every now and then, from far off, puffs of air from the harvested fields, from the dry fallen leaves, from the smell of burning wood. The day's toil was forgotten. Like a bad dream, the day had been. But now night with her eternal breath had come. I heard the soldiers singing and laughing around the fires. The Moroccans, as soon as they saw the stars, lifted up a chant—monotonous, full of grief and passion, like the camel driver's song in the Arabian desert. And suddenly, this whole land of Spain seemed to disappear, with her olive trees and vineyards and her great ill-starred city sleeping near us on the banks of the Manzanares. As that song of the desert passed over her, it devastated her.

I took from my pocket the letter I'd found on the corpse at Getafe. It was from a woman writing to her soldier husband, Francisco López. The letter read:

My darling Francisco!

I had begun to lose heart. I said to myself, something must have happened to him. But then I got your letter and kissed it and screamed for joy.

My darling Francisco, we learn from the newspapers that our side is advancing, and soon the war will be over and you will be coming back to our little house. You never leave my mind, Francisco, my little Francisco, all day long, all night long.

I'm sending you a woolen vest and two pairs of socks. I didn't have anything else. The day before yesterday, Aunt Angelica sent me a bit of orange marmalade, and I'm sending it on to you. I know you love it, and I didn't have the heart to eat it. I'm sending it to you, my little husband, to eat and make your lips sweet. Be careful not to catch cold. . . . Think of our child. Be careful, be careful, my Francisco. Take pity on us. Here, our tiny Carmen wants to tell you, too. She wants to write it to you in her own hand, she says.

(Here the handwriting changes. Thick, uneven letters begin now: most of them in capitals.)

Little papa, please come back. Please, please! Our cat had four kittens. Come and see them.

It's me writing you, I,
Carmen López

▪ MADRID GOES TO HER
DOOM: PART II

▪ "WHERE ARE we going?" I'd asked Unamuno only the day before yesterday.

"To the devil!" he'd answered me.

And indeed, we have entered on an historical era of the insanity of the human race. As happens at critical moments in the evolution of plants and animals, the same insanity is observed throughout the species: anarchy, anxiety, illnesses, short-lived monsters, strange types, until, after much agonized exploring, a new, more perfect species is established; and so life progresses. We are living through a similar insanity of the whole human race. In Spain, I saw horrifying spasms of hatred, heard words that made me shudder, saw children of ten and twelve holding guns and flags. Till all of a sudden, the hate overpowering them had robbed them of the freshness of their youth. They had been transformed into horrible old mannish demons.

Today there is something fearful erupting over the plains and mountains of Spain. A moment of Chaos. A dangerous tornado that is twisting out of control, behind the Pyrenees. Moreover, it is no longer confined to the borders of Spain. The limits and aims of war are gradually being shifted, and with horror we can surmise what lies in store for future generations. I picked up contact with old friends, who had once been calm and good-natured people, devoted to art and science. Now they were unrecognizable. Their eyes gleamed with some uncontrollable lust which was alien to them—lust to burn and kill and torture. This was not their own lust, but the lust of the abominable era we have entered on. The hatred between brothers is dark and primeval. But for thousands of years, it has been quenched. Sometimes, however, it does erupt. And beware of such historical moments! In the course of my present wandering over this Spain that was writhing in such agony, I sensed that the orbit of the earth had moved under the constellation of Cain.

I was trying to discover the pivotal superhuman rhythm that has catalyzed these age-old passions so violently. I know that (as is always true of intense historical moments) all these people, who are finding such pleasure in killing, have lost their individuality. Their faces have been assimilated with the evil demon of our age. They have all donned masks—some red, others black—and rushed out into the arena. They have donned masks and made themselves drunk and changed their natures. When savages don the mask of war, they want to kill. And when they put on their dancing mask, their feet sprout wings and they dance. And when they put on the death mask, they weep. In the same way today, different colored masks are stirring whole races to rage. And behind the enemy's mask, no one can see his own brother's face.

All that night I couldn't sleep. Around daybreak, I saw a dream. I dreamed I was flying a kite, so it seemed. I was holding the string and running from street to street, in a big city. A comfortable breeze was blowing, and the kite was flying with a crackling sound. When I reached the square, I stopped and raised my eyes. And what did I see? It wasn't a kite at all! Flying high in the air, stretched out prone over the rooftops, it had turned into a corpse, all blue-green, with a swollen belly. And out of it dropped little white worms over the roofs and roads and the people's heads.

"The War!" I cried out, waking up with a start.

I went down into the streets. The Moroccans were exultant. Holding their guns tightly and tenderly, they were jumping into their trucks. Grim-looking legionnaires were singing their hymn with hoarse voices. I stood listening to them and had to bite my tongue to keep from crying out.

> *I am a brave and loyal legionnaire,*
> *I am a soldier of a fearless legion.*
> *A sorrow weighs down in my soul*
> *which may be redeemed in fire.*
>
> *My emblem is being fearless,*
> *my fate is only to suffer,*
> *my flag is for fighting bravely*
> *until I conquer or die.*
>
> *Legionnaire, legionnaire,*
> *fight with all you have,*
> *your death may come by chance*
> *for your life is a gamble.*
>
> *Legionnaire, legionnaire*
> *of unequaled bravery,*
> *you will always find a shroud,*
> *legionnaire, under the national flag.*
>
> *Legionnaires, onward to fight!*
> *Legionnaires, onward to die!* *

---

* Translated by Willis Barnstone.

I got into our car, forcing myself to control my excitement. I knew there was no salvation. The sun was bright again today; the sky crystal-clear. The airplanes would be back at work, and I would see one of the loveliest jewels of the earth reduced to ashes. Yesterday the fascist lines had shifted. They were advancing still closer to Madrid, had already set foot in the suburb of Caravanzel. Their embrace was closing in tighter and tighter. Madrid could already feel Franco breathing hot down her neck.

"God has acknowledged the Burgos government!" a priest told me a few days ago. He was wearing the red cap of the Royalists. "See what a sun we have! What a sky! Our airplanes are strong and work well. Our army does not get mud-splashed. The Moroccans are not freezing from the cold. God is with us!"

"*Thou shalt not kill!*" I said to him sarcastically.

"For God, the Fatherland and King!" he answered, highly annoyed.

We were hastily retraversing the broad macabre road—Illiesqua, Torrejon, Parla, Getafe, Alcorcón, Leganés—till we reached Caravanzel. Already this early in the morning, the earth was riddled full of cannon shots. Throngs of soldiers were rushing pell-mell to the front. The Moroccans were shrieking like jackals. The airplanes would be appearing any minute now from wherever they were. Newspaper correspondents from all over the world had gathered here. We climbed the four stories of a big mansion. Furniture, clothes mirrors, photographs, books—all broken, torn, filthy. The table on the fourth floor was still set: the soup still waiting to be served in a big porcelain soup bowl. On the wall there was a big red-and-black stain. I went over to it: blood and hair.

We were perched up on the highest terrace. We'd grabbed

whatever stools, boxes, bundles of clothes, mattresses we could find to sit on. Down there in front of us, just a stone's throw away, so it seemed, lay Madrid: smiling, actual, tangible, and yet on the other side of life, like a mirage. Her streets were deserted today, her windows barred, her public squares empty. Incessantly, mercilessly, rhythmically, the bombs were falling over her. Through our field glasses, we could see a bit of smoke, a leaping movement; a window or wall caving in. She was being smashed to bits. Her divine, sun-washed body was dissolving. The sectors of ashes were growing wider.

I turned around to look at my colleagues. They were all following this bitterest of spectacles, with their field glasses glued to their eyes. I could see their chins and lips and cheeks clearly, and they frightened me: not the tiniest flicker of human compassion on their faces. Some of their lips curled in a sarcastic smile. Some of the others, with their fiercely protruding teeth, looked like dogs ready to bite. And others were just indifferent, cold, remorseless. This industrialized inhuman civilization of ours has made our minds cruel and has withered our hearts. It has made men into scientific barbarians. When men reach this point of inhumanity, it is their destiny (and rightly so!) to become extinct. And this whole Spanish drama, steeped in blood and incoherence and cruelty, is perhaps the prologue (and what is most awful, the justly deserved prologue) to a great catastrophe. I started to cry "Help!" but didn't have time. Behind us, on the farthest point of the horizon, came the sound of airplanes rumbling in the cloudless sky. Everyone up on the terrace began counting away gaily: thirteen, fifteen, nineteen, twenty-one! They were approaching again, three by three—the middle plane leading; the other two, slightly behind. A diabolical and harmonious battle array, a great curving line like cranes.

Only these cranes were not carrying swallows on their wings, but bombs as big as barrels, loaded with death.

"Madrid'll soon be a trainload of ashes," exclaimed a blond newspaper reporter with teeth like a goat's.

He removed his field glasses for a moment, and his eyes flashed, cold, steel-blue, metallical.

I looked at the airplanes rumbling near us now. I looked at Madrid, still heavenly beautiful, with her proud buildings, her churches, her museums, her poor districts so full of human souls. "Goodbye!" I called to her from inside me. "Goodbye!" I was trying to grasp this sun-washed vision of Madrid, to carve it deep in my memory, not to lose her ephemeral form, that it may be preserved inside me as long as I live. It was going to be pulverized a few seconds hence. By now the airplanes were over Madrid. For a second their wings suspended motion, as though in horror.

The interval between this second of apparent suspended motion and the moment when our field glasses showed us a small black dot dropping out of each airplane was longer than a century. A whole century had frozen motionless over us, dense and unbearable. I felt identified with the soul of Madrid. I was lying in wait with her, as she lay there unprotected among the fields, trembling under the twenty-one archangels of this modern apocalypse. I could not think of anything at that moment. I could not even speak a single human word. Even a cry (the deepest, most perfect human expression) was beyond me. This eternity was lightning-swift, and yet I had time to experience all the full horror of life, my own life, the life of Madrid and of the universe. Suddenly terrible cries reverberated from the earth, coming straight from the left bank of the Manzanares, twenty-one times. And at once twenty-one immensely high columns of smoke rose up to the sky. Twenty-one pieces of Madrid, perhaps twenty-one neighborhoods had turned to dust: stones, wood, people scattered to the winds. Madrid was lost behind the clouds of smoke. I was trembling. "What are we going to see now when the clouds of smoke thin?" I said to myself. A gentle breeze was blowing, scattering the smoke. The houses reappeared. They seemed terror-stricken, as though they'd shrunk in their terror. The southern fringe of Madrid was smoking. Tongues of fire darted up, licking the rooftops. Twenty-one holes in her innards. Madrid was losing her finery, falling coal by coal, turning to ashes. The newspapermen near me were jumping up and down in glee. They began applauding.

An officer emerged up on the terrace. I turned around and could hardly restrain myself from crying out: "Saint Maurice!" And in fact, this tall Spaniard, with his pallor and his fine black beard and long ascetic face, looked absolutely like El Greco's ecstatic Saint Maurice in the Escorial. In the sudden fever that had come over Spain, the same bodies had risen again, lit and consumed by the same flame.

"Look," he said. "Look." And he pointed his hand.

On the highway to Valencia, an unending line of cars, trucks, carts. The women and children were fleeing, abandoning Madrid. But who had their minds on the women and children! Through our field glasses, we were all scanning the first districts: the narrow, twisting streets near the Palace and the Plaza de Moros. That was where the terrible battle had exploded. The houses were barred, the windows bolted, and on the streets there were no passers-by. They were no longer using guns: only hand grenades and bayonets, in man-to-man combat.

The pale officer sat down next to me on a stool.

"When will this slaughter end?" I asked him.

"When Madrid, damn her, is ground to ashes."

"And what will you do with her ashes?"

"We'll sow them in the air!" he answered, and his voice trembled with passion.

"And aren't you sorry for her?"

He shrugged his shoulders, then after a short silence: "The Civil War," he murmured, "is a gift of God."

I could no longer bear watching Madrid in her death-throes. I went down into the streets. There was a car transporting three wounded men.

"What's happening?" I asked a young Falange soldier, his hand wounded.

"It's slaughter!" the little soldier answered excitedly. "The devils have gone wild! They've barricaded themselves behind their doors and windows to fire at us. We advance from door to door throwing hand grenades. A hole is made in the wall, and we get into the courtyard. We chase them from room to room, staircase to staircase, floor to floor. 'You're not going to get through! You're not going to pass!' they shout. 'We are so going to pass!' we shout back. And in fact, we have passed."

Passion animated the wounded youngster. He'd started out in a low voice, but now he was getting more and more excited, more and more fierce.

"If I live a thousand years," he cried, "I'll fight a thousand years."

Trucks and cars kept arriving, full of wounded men. They were all radiant, as though the bullet had hit them at a moment of intense pleasure. Their faces glowed strangely, like the faces of dancers. The whole secret of war is to be overwhelmingly drunk. Then fear vanishes. Life and death appear the same. A delectable longing governs men to annihilate and be annihilated: to cease to exist. This violent excitement is capable of transforming danger into pleasure. Mutilation and death exist on a plane utterly removed from our usual lives, where such spectacles evoke horror. Alas for the fighting man who is not drunk, though! For to him, everything becomes a nightmare, terror, panic.

More trucks and cars were arriving again, overflowing with more wounded soldiers. The Moroccans had thronged here, fleeing from Toledo. There were also legionnaires and taciturn officers. Violent unrest in the air.

"What's going on?" I asked an officer friend of mine, Major Rubio, whom I'd known in Toledo, and who had just arrived. He too was very upset.

"What's going on? But don't you understand?" he answered me. "Yesterday, the first phase of the war ended: the romantic. Today, the second, the realistic, is beginning. The first called for impatience, high spirits, impetuosity. This second phase demands patience, gravity, endurance. Now the Reds have penetrated Madrid. Each of them is fortified inside his own house: Captain Sole. He knows the streets, the neighbors, the hiding places. He piles mattresses in front of his window, hides behind them and shoots. His wife is there to help him, bring him food and water and cartridges. At night he can sleep. He doesn't get cold. He doesn't get wet. He doesn't suffer. Now the terrible chase has begun, from street to street and house to house. Yes, they're resisting like mad. But we'll get past them!"

Victory had finally been set on the elevated dangerous plane befitting it, had become the far-off Cordova of the poet Lorca. Or the red apple Sappho speaks of, shining high up at the very top of the apple tree, there because the pickers hadn't been able to reach it—the inaccessible blood-red apple, bathed in the sun and the rains.

■ ■

When I went back to Toledo that evening, once again, I saw Cupid walking the streets like a vagabond. New regiments of Moroccans had arrived. The streets and wine shops and cafés were crowded. The radios had begun blaring, trying to infuse courage. But tonight the faces were anxious and overcast. At the main gate to the bishop's residence, a Spanish friend of mine stopped me.

"You know," he said to me, "they've killed the poet you used to love. . . ."

"Who?" I shuddered with horror.

"Federico García Lorca."

"Lorca! Who killed him?"

"Some say the Reds. Others say we did. Nobody knows for sure."

"Why not?"

"I don't know. Maybe there was some misunderstanding," he added, shrugging his shoulders.

As in Shakespeare's tragedies, people are killed like this for no reason. Life hangs by a thread and this thread is tolled back and forth in the hands of blind and conscienceless fate. Because of a similarity of names; or because of a word that was never actually uttered; or because of wearing the same clothes as someone else.

In Zocodover Square, the radios were blaring: "We've taken . . . We've taken . . . We've driven out . . . We've captured . . . We're advancing . . ." But the faces were overcast. And Cupid was roaming the narrow little streets, standing at the street corners, stirring up the soldiers who would be leaving for the front tomorrow. But even Cupid had a sullen expression now. More violent, more hurried and unsmiling. Hands and bodies and souls seemed to have separated, aware that they might never meet again. Poe's immortal raven sat perched on everyone's shoulder again: "Nevermore! Nevermore!" And all Toledo reverberated, filled with a mysterious exciting scent of ashes and sweat.

I pushed on toward the Cathedral. On the way, a tall soldier with a black beard grabbed a woman as he was passing— at random. He dragged her by the arm. The woman resisted, laughing. But the soldier pulled irresistibly and mercilessly; slowly, hungrily caressing the unfamiliar arm.

"*Venga! Venga! Venga!*" he whispered to her. "Come with me! Come on! Come on!"

The woman giggled nervously as though he were tickling her. And her mantilla tumbled. *Venga! Venga! Venga!* I was watching the scene eagerly, worried that the woman might refuse. I was delighted by the violence of these embraces made in the shadow of death. Life is apparently afraid of becoming extinct, and so rouses our poor obedient flesh to double duty. Whoever is killed in battle is replaced instantaneously in a single night.

It was cold. In the tiny garden next door to the Cathedral, there was a hut, a kerosene lamp lit, and a woman roasting chestnuts. I was attracted by their pleasant smell and rushed over to fill my hands gaily with hot chestnuts. There was a little girl standing next to me, chewing away.

"Is she your child?" I asked.

"Ah *señor*," the woman answered me with a sigh. "I am *soltera*, unmarried."

She must have been about thirty years old. Bony, prematurely aged, the complaining type.

"*Soltera!*" I said, suddenly frightened. "And why?"

"Ah *señor*, nobody wants me. . . . Nobody, *señor*. Nobody. But now with the war . . ."

She smiled and stopped talking.

"What?" I asked. "What?"

"Ah, some war cripple will turn up to take me. . . ."

This made me happy, as though some well-loved friend of mine had escaped from danger. This chestnut-woman looked on the war as a kind-hearted old matchmaker, who'd mounted his mule and traveled from far off to knock on her little hut and bring her a wedding ring. I ate the hot chestnuts happily as I roamed about Toledo. I kept thinking of this chestnut-woman whose breasts would soon flow with milk, thanks to the war.

■ THE MULTI-COLORED CAPS

■ RESTLESS, NERVOUS, the multi-colored caps were circulating through the streets of Toledo: red, black, green, blue. In the darkness the Cathedral glimmered, enormously high and threatening. In the air I breathed some indefinable terror. A throng of *requetes* passed by, their large bodies exuding comfort and ease. They were singing their hymn:

> *March on, Red Caps,*
> *For the Holy Faith!*
> *March on, Red Caps,*
> *For an immortal Spain!*

They had one grand cause: the monarchy. But who was their candidate for monarch? I asked and asked again. They just coughed and answered nothing:

"Alfonso?"

"God forbid! He's illegitimate on the female side of the Bourbons."

"Well, who is it then? Carlos? But he died a few months ago in Vienna, at the age of eighty-seven!"

The *requetes* would cough again:

"What a man!" he'd exclaim, gesticulating in the air. "What a horseman! Why, just imagine, when he was eighty-five, he could still mount his horse in one leap."

"Yes . . . but now?"

The *requetes* would hem and haw once more; then with infinite politeness he'd take his leave.

In exasperation, I rushed to the *requetes* headquarters. It was an old palace. I climbed staircases and side staircases, losing my way in the corridors. I asked one of the chiefs. He would be sure to know. All of them were eager and extremely polite, but just sent me on from person to person, and office to office. At last I found a jolly man about forty years old; he was wearing a lavender-colored tassel.

"I refuse to leave unless you give me an answer," I said to him laughingly. "Help me understand what it is you want and what your program is."

"Don Rodrigos Morales knows all this sort of stuff better. Let me take you to him!"

"No! No! It's Don Rodrigos who just sent me to Your Excellency."

The chief sank back in his chair with a discreet sigh.

"I'm at your service!" he said, screwing up his face.

"Well, first of all, I'd like to learn how and why Carlism came into being in Spain," I told him.

The historical information of the chief was a bit shaky. He couldn't remember dates.

"In 1858 . . ." he started to say. "In 1870 . . . well, some time around then."

He couldn't remember names either. Every so often, he ran out to the corridor to question various passers-by. When he came back, breathlessly, he'd bring me a date or a name. But soon he'd stumble once more.

"*Perdón!*" he'd beg me, as he flew out to the hall again.

At last we got clear of history and approached politics. The *requetes* caught fire. His face turned as scarlet as his cap. He lowered his voice ceremoniously.

"Liberties were handed to the people, and this is where we've ended up: chaos! But this error will not be made again! We shall offer a monarch who'll swear to follow our sacred tradition. He will give no liberties!"

"Who?" I asked, looking him straight in the eye, so he couldn't get away from me.

The *requetes* began to turn this over in his mind. He produced an array of dukes, princes, Bourbons and finally reached an unexpected conclusion:

"The most likely is the third son of Alfonso: Don Juan."

"But haven't we already said that he's illegitimate on his mother's side of the family!" I insisted, maliciously.

The *requetes* jumped up, blushing bright red. He was a most polite *hidalgo*, however, and controlled himself.

"If I can be of use to you in anything else . . ." he said.

But I refused to let him get away.

"What stand do you take on present-day social and economic problems?" I asked in a calm voice, as pleasantly as I could manage.

"*Hombre!*" he answered explosively. "Not so fast! It's not the time yet for such details. But we do love the poor," he added, as he straightened his tassel. "We are Catholics, and the religion of Christ . . ."

On the way back, I met an old newspaper acquaintance of mine: a widely traveled very well-informed man, but a miserable wretch of a fellow, with a passion for eating and drinking. At another period, he'd stayed for years in Spain. He'd been an *aficionado* of the bullfights. And now, he went to the Front with a pair of military field glasses. And when some offensive move pleased him, he began applauding and throwing his bowler hat up in the air. Then, in the evening, he'd get into his car and rush off to the nearest public square, where he could bathe himself luxuriously and drink some whisky. And now I saw him in a bar, drinking. He beckoned to me. I went in. He laughed at me for not drinking whisky and not wearing a hat. "We ought to wear hats," he said to me, "so we can throw them in the air whenever we're feeling enthusiastic!"

Tonight, the second I entered the bar:

"Where're you coming from?" he asked me. "You look tired."

I explained my troubles to him, and he burst out laughing.

"You're incorrigible!" he exclaimed. "You've come here armed with pen and paper. But you're only going to upset these poor innocent beasts who've never yet suffered from the terrible disease of thought. Can't you understand that everything that's happening here is what the Bedouins call 'fantasia.' A Bedouin sits motionless for hours on end, staring out at the desert. Suddenly his heart bursts. He feels suffocated. If he's a poor man, he grabs a box of matches and burns them all at once. He watches the fire, and his spirit feels lighter. If he's rich, he rides his horse, dashes into the village, galloping up and down, with his white jelab floating in the air. And if a whole race is involved, it makes war. The Spaniards are burning their boxes of matches, riding their horses, making war. That's all. . . ."

But that shrewd old man was not right. The agony convulsing Spain is something deeper, more tragic than the Bedouin *fantasia*. Perhaps the ideologies of the *requetes* are out of date. But they do have a passionate will. And what counts in a struggle is not the ideology, but the rhythm and idiosyncrasy of the people who are struggling. In the statutes of their order, the following commands are listed:

1. Be a faultless horseman.
2. Know how to obey in a disciplined way.
3. Preserve your name untainted.
4. Always be prepared to face danger.
5. Never make compromises or sacrifice your ideal.
6. Be never tepid; ever self-possessed.
7. Suffer silently the cold and heat, hunger, thirst, illness, pains and fatigue.

The members of the Falange are still more impassioned. Their ideology is more clearly defined; and they are more organized, more energetic, more attuned to present-day needs. They have companies, divisions, regiments, leaders. The spirit that moves them is warlike. Here are the five main commands of the Falange legionnaire:

1. The legionnaire must always bear in mind that prison, wounds and death are an integral part of his service.
2. The hard persistent service of the legionnaire is an honor, not forced labor. Only those who are worthy of such an honor may serve the Falange.
3. The brave deeds of the legionnaire are not publicized. Only his shortcomings are reported.
4. The legionnaire must obey his superior unconditionally. At whatever hour of the day or night he is summoned, he must go quickly and eagerly.
5. Obedience is the fundamental virtue of the legionnaire. Joyous obedience, without ostentation or ambition.

A large hall; brightly lit; midnight. A bunch of very young legionnaires, dark-skinned, short, poor-looking. When they'd gotten their orders, they jumped into the cars and rode off.

"I want to see 'Comrade' Rafael Garzerán," I told the sentry.*

"*Ordenanza!*" the tiny soldier bellowed, sending a soldier to ask for the permit.

I looked carefully at the sentry. He was slender. His body wasn't yet fully fledged. He had a childlike tenderness.

"How old are you, Comrade?"

"Sixteen."

"So young!"

"I'm not young!" He seemed upset. "I'm sixteen years old."

I'd forgotten. Nowadays each year is momentous, concentrated, eventful. Nowadays men are familiar with wine and cigarettes and women, from the time they are young boys. Sometimes they have known even murder. Just a few days ago, hadn't a lad told me proudly: "I've killed people, too!" Abruptly, without having passed through the springtime season of shyness and innocence, the babies are turned into grown men.

The orderly came back.

"Enter!" the little soldier said in an official little voice.

The head of the Falange shut the door and the hubbub died down. He was about thirty years old, short and robust. The nape of his neck and his arms were very fat. He moved with quick sudden gestures: the *toreador* type. His eyes were blue, flashing like steel. This generous corpulent body seemed to be nourishing a strong fierce will.

He plunged right in, in a thundering voice: "Of the three causes—God, Fatherland, and King—we are prepared to fight to the death for only one: the Fatherland. But not such a Fatherland as in the past, when the common people were left

---

* Among themselves the Falange soldiers are called "comrades."

to rot away in poverty and wallow in blind ignorance. We want a just Fatherland that will protect everyone—rich and poor, high-born and commoners alike, without any privileged class."

The more he talked, the more his eyes flashed. The veins in his fat neck puffed. The *toreador* in him was roused.

"No!" he roared, having difficulty in keeping himself from striking his fist on the table. "No! We have not been making war and sending hundreds of thousands of Falange men to die just to fatten the rich people's bellies and let the common people fall back into their wretched condition! Victory has given us rights, and we shall not allow anyone to take them from us. If need be, we'll go back onto the streets again and fight."

He got up and strode around the room a few times to calm down.

"We men of the Falange are not a political party. We're a military regiment. We want to introduce a new social justice, an economic order that will be above class interests. We want to abolish the political parties, the Catholic suffrage, elections, parliamentary cliques. We want a strong government that will be neither capitalistic nor Marxist. All the powers of production will form a single organized entity within the framework of the government. There will be no disorder in production; no injustice in the distribution of wealth. Land will be given to the peasants, justice and bread to the laborers, reading and writing to everyone. You see, we want to create a new Fatherland. Who knows, perhaps a new conception of life. . . . You may say, but this is fascism. Correct. And then you might ask me, what are the Spanish overtones of fascism? But how can you expect us to know them at this point? For they are not abstract ideologies; no geometric forms on paper. They are actual practice: the result of painful, long-drawn-out experimentation. Little by little our own way, the Spanish way, will be forged. Come back to us after a few years, or a few generations, and then we'll be able to answer your question. For the answer does not yet exist. It is coming into being."

These words of the young Falange chief were engraved on my mind when I left. And more than his words: the expression on his face, the tone of his voice, the fire in his eyes. I sensed hundreds of thousands of young people all over the world today talking through his lips.

The next day early in the morning, a flock of new caps emerged in Zocodover Square. Freshly pressed, bright green, with a red cross in the shape of a sword hilt. The Spaniards are thrilled by discord. Each one loves to hoist his own colors, wear his own distinctive cap, embroidered with a cross different from the next man's cross: "Our cross is for Saint Jacob of Compostela!" the Green Caps exclaim proudly. "Ours is the cross of Isabella!" others say, with imperialistic hauteur. "Ours is the cross of Saint Andrew!" A bit more and the crosses start quarreling among themselves, quite forgetting the Crucified Saviour.

I started questioning a short plump little Green Cap, who was about to go into the Cathedral.

"We're the *Renovación Española*," he answered me. "The Spanish Renaissance!"

"But nowadays, everyone is asking for the Renaissance of Spain," I said to him. "What distinguishes you from the rest of them?"

"We're very different! We, my friend, are Monarchists!"

"Like the *requetes!*" I said.

"No! No! Absolutely different! Our leader is Don Antonio."

"But in other respects, you're in agreement with the *requetes?*"

"Not at all! Not at all!" (He seemed terrified by the notion of their possible agreement.) "We want to put Alfonso XIII on the throne, and they're Carlists . . ."

"But their Carlos is dead. I don't imagine they want to put a corpse on the throne?"

My interlocutor laughed:

"You see!" he exclaimed triumphantly. "You see! We have a living man to put on the throne. There's our advantage!"

"And what's your social program? You'll offer an up-to-date solution to contemporary economic and social problems?"

"Oh, absolutely!" he answered, raising his hand as though swearing an oath. "We're absolutely up-to-date! We intend to follow our medieval tradition. We'll bring back the Monarchy and the Cortes. This is what our history dictates! This is what our souls dictate! This is what must happen! And it shall happen!"

With this rhetorical fanfare, he sprang up and went into the church.

I sat down on a bench facing the Cathedral. The light was streaming down over its stone saints and angels and gargoyles. Up over the rooftops, they emerged gazing down on the people below. Without understanding why, I thought of Lorca's fierce verses:

> *Life is not a dream! Rise up! Arise!*
> *We are being catapulted down the stairs.*
> *One day horses will inhabit the wine*
> *shops. And the maddened ants will climb*
> *the yellow heavens.*

There was an old man sitting next to me on the bench. He wore a new red cross sewn on his chest and a pale blue cap.

"What are you, neighbor?" I asked him.

"*Albinianos!*" he answered proudly.

"*Albinianos?* What's that?"

"A Catholic Monarchist!"

"Like the *requetes*," I asked, "and the *Renovación Española?*"

"No! No!" the old man protested. "We have another leader."

"Who?"

"Albiniates."

"Where is he now? I'd like to see him and have him explain his program . . ."

"Ouf! How could you see the poor man now! He died in prison several months ago. The Reds killed him. They chopped him into small pieces—mincemeat!"

"And this mincemeat is your leader?"

"Yes!" the old man answered, fiercely and fanatically. "Yes . . . this mincemeat!"

"And what's your social program?"

"Our what?"

"Your social program . . ."

The old man scratched his head.

"A friend of mine has it," he said after a long pause.

I got up and walked along the uphill path behind the Cathedral, till I reached the old building that had once housed the horrific Palace of the Holy Inquisition. The outer gate is still intact, a marvel of elegance and power: exceedingly high and slender, made of marble. Over the lintel, Isabella the Great's coat-of-arms is carved. And to the right and left of it, her two emblems: a scale and a cluster of darts bound in the shape of an open fan—the same emblems chosen some five centuries later by the Falange. At the very top of the gate is another coat-of-arms, held in place by a bat, whose ratlike head, with a halo around it, is still clearly visible.

Today the Palace of the Holy Inquisition has turned into a *posada*, or inn. The "Inn of the Brotherhood." Mules, filth, darkness!

"Come in, come in!" the innkeeper invited me, the image of politeness in the midst of all this filth.

I entered, holding my nose as I moved through the huge old ground-floor areas. Nowadays, mules eat here and hungry pigs trot to and fro. I climbed the heavy stone staircase up to the first floor—the official chamber where the awesome and omnipotent Inquisitioners used to convene. Today the floor is full of holes and unmentionable filth. Over in a corner, a flock of ragged peasants had lain down to sleep. On the walls, red and blue tints are still visible from faded wall paintings.

■ MANOLA: CALIBAN

■ THE DAYS ARE passing. We are no longer allowed to go to the Front. People's faces are growing more and more sullen. Victory has closed her bloodstained wings and is standing motionless between the two armies. When I went down to Zocodover Square, a freezing wind was blowing. In the gray early morning light, the Alcázar glowed pale, full of grief, as though repentant. "I must go now . . . must go away," I was thinking to myself. I walked around the square to find Julio, my driver. Somewhere there he'd be sipping at his wine and cursing Madrid in bitter plaintive words, as though she were his unfaithful but beloved wife.

I stared at the mascots that the Spanish drivers had stuck on their cars and trucks: embalmed eagles, owls, monstrous dolls, fierce masks painted in red and yellow. A jungle of wild animals, age-old gods, who suddenly at the hour of danger are dragged up from the depths of human memory. Man, like a poor wretch, resurrects them and cries to them for help! Everyone has some animal inside himself: an ancient god of his own generation. And at the critical moment, he brings this god forth into the light. Deep within them, the Spaniards must have one of the most monstrous of pantheons.

"Julio, we're going!"

He was sitting in a wine shop, drinking by himself. He got up, looking at me with sad eyes.

"Well, will it be long before she falls, *caballero?*"

"Have a happy spring!" I murmured to him.

We're off: Avila, Salamanca, Valladolid, Burgos, Irún. . . .

Julio sighed, made the sign of the cross, set his horrid mascot doll right side up, and we started off.

We are leaving the heroic ruins in our wake—the heroes of the Alcázar, the mystic visions of El Greco. . . . A serene plain; peacefulness; the sun emerging among the clouds, shedding light on the ploughed fields; scattered army boots; upside-down wrecks of trucks; dead horses. And further on, at the Front, the Reds and the Blacks. . . . The ruined villages had begun filling up again. Women emerged on their doorsteps, laughing and bustling about as though there were no war going on. In the public square of one village, there was a sign: "The Jesus Barber Shop." Up on the balcony, a sheet was spread out, and in the middle of it was a big red splotch of paint that looked like a pear.

"That's the heart of Jesus," my driver explained to me.

Beyond the village, a forked road branched off. There was a pale young man sunning himself in the door of a long house. His legs were covered with a red blanket.

"Hey!" the driver called to him. "Hey, kinsman, come over here a minute."

But the kinsman shook his head.

"You come here!" he answered back.

The driver got angry.

"Aren't you ashamed of yourself! There's a foreigner here!" he said, pointing to me.

But then the villager lifted the blanket—his two legs had been chopped off!

We took the road to the right. Poplar trees rising in the sunlight, their two or three leaves up on top, shimmering golden. I turned around. From several of the houses the chimneys were smoking with a peacetime smoke. Beneath the dilapidated roofs, the people were cooking. Man and wife were once again sitting and eating at each other's side. They would gather their forces again. In the evenings they would sleep together. They would give birth to new children. Perhaps new flesh for more cannon. . . . But at the sublime moment of creation, who stops to ponder on logic and death?

In another village, we stopped to eat at a *posada*. The lady innkeeper was a short, fine-boned old woman, with big eyes. In her youth she must have been a dangerous beauty; must have caused many stilettos to flash by sun and moonlight. Now they called her Aunt Juanita. She brought us some boiled eggs, peppers, and a watermelon. She hovered near us, hungry for conversation. Then she began telling stories, horrible stories, in an almost nonchalant tone of voice, devoid of anger or grief. She seemed to be talking about things from the remote past.

"Here, in this doorway, they killed my husband. Over there the priest. . . . They collected twenty-five of our most well-to-do men, crammed them into a truck, sprayed gasoline and set them on fire!"

The more she chattered, the gayer Aunt Juanita got. She warmed up. Her cheeks turned rosy.

"What do you think, Aunt Juanita? Will all those murderers go to Hell?"

"To Hell?" the old woman exclaimed in surprise. "Why? Maybe they feel sorry after they've killed. If you kill someone and then look at him and say, 'Ay *pobrecito!* Oh, the poor man!' God will forgive you."

"But is that enough, Aunt Juanita? Ay *pobrecito?*"

"It's enough, child! It's enough!" she said, patting me on the shoulder as though to soothe me.

After the main food, we cut the watermelon. There was a refreshing whiff of the sea.

"Goodbye, Aunt Juanita! . . . If I had enough time, as I used to in past years, I would have stayed here two or three days and nights to listen to you tell me all about your youth—all the men who used to come down from the mountainsides with their red belts and broad *sombreros* and their gaily saddled mules, riding down to knock on your door . . . But now, where to find the time, Aunt Juanita!"

A flock of women had collected around us. They were shoving and elbowing each other in their eagerness to speak, each one dying to talk about her own troubles and ease her heart. Such is the bitter and incurable human weakness: to sit and bare one's heart to each and every passer-by, without pride or shame. I met only one old man who refused to prattle about his grief. He was sitting in front of his ruined hovel, rocking an empty cradle slowly and with great care. His eyes stared with a glazed expression into the empty cradle. They were absolutely dry.

"What's the matter, old man?" I asked him. "What have they done to you?"

The old man lifted his head, casting an angry look at me:

"Go to the devil!" he snarled at me.

And I was happy, because I had encountered a proud spirit.

Navalcarnero . . . San Martín . . . Zembreros. There was a café full of soldiers, all of them young—twenty years old— eating and drinking. They brought us some of the superb wine of Zembreros, and we drank with them. Twenty years old, and they'd already lived and suffered like men a hundred years old. They were talking with strange sadistic relish about all they'd seen: killing, martyrdom, bloodshed. They all talked about death, as though it were some country near here, just opposite Spain, where they were all going, one by one. And I didn't hear a single word to indicate that it is a terrifying country, one from which there is no return.

"Enough of the dead now, fellows!" called a dark lad, with cheeks still smooth and downy. "Take your chairs out of the middle of the floor. Carlito, you sing! And I'll dance!"

A black-haired Moroccan, the spitting image of him, opened his huge mouth and began singing the "Canta Junto"—the old Arabic song of Andalusia. With his head thrown back, soaking in sweat, he was carried away by the pathetic refrain of his Moorish ancestors. And as he sang it, all Africa sang through his lips, savagely, erotically. The first soldier began to dance. Love, war, woman, death fused and became one in his mad whirling dance. Their legs quivered and they all leaped up and started dancing. As the little tassels on their colored caps shook and their bright blanket-capes flapped around them, they looked just like woodcocks in the springtime, dancing in the forest before the female bird. All the horror of the war suddenly disappeared. War had found its original face again: bloodstained, drunk, intensely cruel, but without malice.

By evening we'd reached Avila. A strange ferment seethed in the streets. Everyone's face glowed, as though reflecting some great fire.

"What's going on?" I asked.

"Franco arrived today!" came their answer.

Suddenly the faces of the opulent and well-to-do, usually so empty of light and fire, take on a glow when some fiery spirit passes near them. Without understanding it, they are overwhelmed by a fever: admiration, love—above all, fear. And their eyes catch fire.

In the restaurant where I went to eat dinner, I met a lieutenant acquaintance of mine: Hernandez. He laughed when I told him about the macabre, yet hilarious talk of the Zembreros soldiers.

"The word 'sorry' I've never once heard on any Spaniard's lips," I remarked. "Quite the contrary! Once someone actually said to me: 'For the Spaniards, the Civil War is a gift of God!' "

"Yes, I know," said Hernandez, laughing. "Only a Spaniard could sense the meaning of this terrible phrase. But surely, when you arrived in Spain, you must also have been aware of some inexplicable feverish exultation. As though all the Spaniards, both the Right and the Left, had at last found what they were looking for."

"The violent gestures; the bloody spectacles; the war?"

"Yes. . . . The highest form of the bullfight. Before I put on this uniform to go and fight, I did other work. I was a teacher in a village in Asturia. I looked and listened and spoke with the people; ate and drank with them; loved them. They loved me too. Often the workingmen used to come to me to tell me their complaints. Most of them had stopped going to church, and I became a sort of father confessor to them. I was amazed when I heard what these Spanish souls had to confess to me. In this way, little by little, I was led to ponder on what this race of ours is supposed to be: full of its violent impulses and incurable wrath. And I reached the following conclusion . . ."

For a moment the officer hesitated.

"I don't know if I'm right," he finally went on, "but this is my opinion: The Spaniard has many souls inside himself.

He is a mixture of many races that are still uncrystallized, that are full of contradictory desires. All these conflict inside him and never leave him in peace. He loves life passionately. But at the same time, a cry stirs inside him: 'All this is nothing!' All at once, he no longer fits in anywhere, and he yearns for death. His soul is catapulted suddenly from one extreme to the other. Even the mildest Spaniard suffers like a martyr inside himself. And in order not to see or hear all that is going on inside him, he has an organic need to burst out in violence and bloodshed. He is like a person with too much blood from whom they must take blood. Here's the explanation of this Civil War of ours and the inhuman joy it gives us. Yes, of course, economic causes also play an important role, I don't forget that. But for Spain, these are only excuses. These are the keys that open the menagerie inside him. But once the primordial passions have burst, the struggle is no longer controlled by economic causes or great ideas. It is then controlled by passion. And the Spaniard's passion has a most bitter root: despair."

I was very upset by his words. A whole swarm of dark things I hadn't been able to explain were now clarified, in a nauseating, yet clear light. I went up to my room to be alone. I couldn't sleep. So many unexpected contradictory impressions vexing the mind, compelling it to intervene. Now that my painful adventure here is drawing to a close, I must try to catalogue the events I have lived and make order of the chaos.

> The Spaniards are killing each other like age-old enemies—as though, for centuries, grudges and vendettas have been mounting inside them. Now the terrible moment has come, and their souls have found relief. They feel lighter.

The two fatal words, "Red" and "fascist," are not the cause of the present hatred. They are only one of the historical excuses the Spaniards always invent for bursting out and relieving themselves.

What is the dark force consuming them? The Spaniards are pre-eminently an African race. For years on end, they crouch motionless, watching and listening and longing. Their hearts are like a cistern of water: suddenly they overflow. And then warfare, dangerous adventures, civil upheaval come like the gifts of some bloodthirsty god, enabling them to find relief. They find relief, use up their surplus energy, and then return to their natural quiescence.

Of course, other dark forces also intervene. Above all, two: Hunger and Injustice. Social injustice in Spain is intolerable. For centuries, the peasants cultivated their overlords' farms, poured their sweat and their blood onto the land . . . and went hungry.

But then one day, all the wronged and hungry ones sprang up and seized power—in the elections last February. Great and exaggerated expectations were based on this victory. But, immediately after the victory, the victors, united so long as they were fighting their common enemy, began quarreling among themselves: Communists, socialists, anarchists.

As was natural in Spain, the anarchists prevailed. Strikes, murders, arson broke out. The various provinces raised their heads, demanding separation, independence. Spain was in danger of falling to pieces.

The opposition centripetal forces—Catholics and monarchists, military and patriotic—organized themselves. On the 18th of July, the revolution broke out. The mortal clash began.

Who will win? Whoever the victor is, if he means to ensure his victory, he must introduce and establish two main virtues in Spain: discipline, whether by force or by kindness, in whatever way he is able. And social justice: the peasant must be emancipated from his feudal lord and must have enough food. Laws favorable to the workers must be legislated. The Church must be kept out of every sphere outside the Church. The people must be educated.

Will the future victors want or have time to do this? If my personal opinion is worth mentioning I would answer unhesitantly: "No!"

I am sitting alone, musing, in this deserted corner of Avila. I feel unbearably sad for this pathetic lovable country that has seen so much bloodshed. Not even three years have passed since I had roamed through her cities and villages. It had been springtime then. "*All the air was a bird,*" and Argentina was dancing with a red rose in her raven hair. Now Argentina had changed to La Pasionara, and the rose into a deep red wound. And Azaña as I'd known him then —smiling, ironical, sure of himself—now rose like a pale

full-moon mask: an impotent hero of some murderous tragedy. Someone who'd seen him recently had told me: "He's
aged, grown old. These last months have wasted him away.
His brain sees all the mistakes crystal-clear. He cries out, but
who is there to listen to him?" We have entered the twen-
tieth century, dark, terrifying, iron-clad. Poor Azaña goes on
as a Democrat of the happy past. When he assumed the
tragic role as President of the Republic, he proclaimed: "I
shall be a President incorruptible either by the extreme
Right or the extreme Left. . . ." He judged badly. For he
lacked the personal power, and even more, because he failed
to grasp that no human force is capable of checking the historical cataclysm we face today, that is pushing us inevitably
either to the extreme Right or the extreme Left. He forgot
that the genuine role of the politician is not to stop history,
but to work in harmony with it. For life is no emotional
affair, no pro- or anti-freedom ideology. It is an awesome
force, unafraid of bloodshed.

It was nearly daybreak. For a moment I fell asleep, and as
usual, the agony and struggle of the preceding day continued. I saw a terrible dream: Argentina was dancing, her head
scraping the ground in a strange state, shaking her flounces
in the air, striking her heels against the stones, shouting in
her hoarse voice: "Olé! Olé! Olé!" And suddenly she lifted
her head high . . . and it was a death skull!

I jumped up. It was dawn. The ravens of Avila were croak-
ing, and the ghost of Argentina had vanished. Pale but gay,
the autumnal light laughed against the windowpanes. Once
again, my heart felt resilient. I no longer cared about dead
Argentinas or the desperate fate of Azaña. I got into the car,
continuing my trek northward. And the courageous verses of
a Madrilenian poet, Heraldo Diego, ambled over my lips:

With broken boards and old bricks
and crumbled stones, let us reconstruct
our world! The page is blank—"In the
beginning was . . ."

But the page is not white. It is deep red. Such, however, is the color first pages always have in history.

We are leaving Avila behind us, passing through Salamanca, moving on to Valladolid. The higher we go, the darker the sky grows. It has begun to rain. We are passing villages and ruined towers and bridges. The poplars have lost their leaves and are trembling naked in the air. In the villages and cities, men, women, children are reading the bulletins posted on the walls; listening to the radio; leaning over their newspapers. Eager, anxious, at a high peak of concentration. At other periods, these same people had been asleep, hungry and taciturn, rolling about the cafés in boredom. Now—thanks to this horrible war!—all the Spaniards, both Rightists and Leftists, have woken up. Habit, indifference, routine are no longer molding the Spanish destiny. All the Spaniards are actively taking part, demanding to share in the Responsibility. Time has assumed importance and value. . . .

One day several years ago, in Seville, I'd seen a young man. He was about twenty-five years old, pale, with dark whiskers. There he lay stretched out in the sunlight, his eyes half-closed, looking calmly, lazily, sensually at the passers-by.

"That's Manola!" my Spanish friend laughed as he told me. "All day long he lies there stretched out in the sun. He doesn't want to work, even if it means he has to die of hunger."

I went up to him.

"Ah, Manola!" I called to him. "They tell me you're hungry. Why don't you get up and work? Aren't you ashamed of yourself?"

Manola stirred sluggishly, then raised his hand with king-like grandeur:

"*En la hambre mando yo!*" he answered me. "In hunger I am King!"

As though hunger were some boundless kingdom, and so long as Manola remained hungry, he kept the scepter of this kingdom in his own hands. To have done the slightest bit of work, to have eaten the slightest bit of food, would have meant the loss of his royalty.

"Will his life just go to the dogs like this?" I asked my friend.

But my friend laughed:

"If Manola rises up," he said, "woe betide us!"

Well, Manola, Caliban, has risen up. He has gotten sick of his crown of hunger. He has dressed himself as a soldier: Communist, anarchist, Falange member, *requetes, regulares.* Life has changed its rhythm. Hunger, injustice, misery, as usual, have been transformed into terrifying explosive forces. We are going through the dangerous, time-consuming, unstable period of transition, steeped in experiment, enthusiasm, bitterness. This is how humanity has always progressed from one form of political and social life to the next. Whoever wants to be able to bear, and, more than bear, to justify the horror of the present moment, must see beyond the present moment to the future. He must overcome his sensitivity. He must realize that such has always been the course over the earth of the so-called Spirit, whose feet have always been sunk in bloodshed and mud.

By now, we are up overlooking Burgos. A wild landscape: bare oak trees, sheer gray rocks. A driving rain had been beating down on them and they are all sparkly. The sun is setting among blood-red clouds. There is something horrifying and inhuman spreading in the air. And suddenly a savage memory floats into my mind. In a ruined village near Toledo, I had seen the soldiers burning books, photographs, newspapers in the public square and dancing gleefully around them, as though they were burning people alive. I had caught sight of a colored lithograph, and quickly bent over the flames to grab it: the "Cronos" of Goya!

Cronos—his eyes glazed, his mouth gaping—is crushing a tiny doll-size child in his hands. As he eats it, there is blood streaming down his beard. His lips are scarlet, swollen with voracity and lust.

And now in these final moments as I am leaving Spain, this Cronos springs up in my memory and I look on him in terror. "Who has seen the face of Spain's God?" Antonio Machado cries out in one of his songs. "My heart awaits the hard-handed Iberian to carve on the Castilian oak the God of Spain!" But surely Cronos is not her eternal God. However many of his children he may eat, there will always be one left to bring a new rhythm to the world. Who will this future God be, this lucky son of Cronos?

Let us give no answer to this. Let us close our bloody sojourn in Spain with the verses of the great lyric poet, Juan Ramón Jiménez:

> I take my hope, like a shining
> diamond, from its sheath, my heart.
> I walk with it among the roses, caress
> it as a daughter, as a sister, as my
> mistress. Hungrily I worship it, then
> lock it up again alone.